rbl
The RBL Group

www.rbl.net

HOW GREAT LEADERS BUILD
ABUNDANT ORGANIZATIONS
THAT WIN

THE *why* OF work

DAVE ULRICH
WENDY ULRICH

New York   Chicago   San Francisco   Lisbon   London   Madrid   Mexico City
Milan   New Delhi   San Juan   Seoul   Singapore   Sydney   Toronto

The McGraw·Hill Companies

1 2 3 4 5 6 7 8 9 10 11 12 13 14 15 16   WFR/WFR   1 9 8 7 6 5 4 3 2 1 0

ISBN   978-0-07-173935-1
MHID   0-07-173935-1

This publication is designed to provide accurate and authoritative information in regard to the subject matter covered. It is sold with the understanding that the publisher is not engaged in rendering legal, accounting, securities trading, or other professional services. If legal advice or other expert assistance is required, the services of a competent professional person should be sought.
>   —From a Declaration of Principles Jointly Adopted by a Committee of the
>   American Bar Association and a Committee of Publishers and Associations

Interior design by Think Bookworks

McGraw-Hill books are available at special quantity discounts to use as premiums and sales promotions or for use in corporate training programs. To contact a representative, please e-mail us at bulksales@mcgraw-hill.com.

This book is printed on acid-free paper.

CONTENTS

FOREWORD

Why? What is the why behind *The Why of Work?* Why should you read this book? Why should you care?

In 1979, my largest leadership development client was IBM, which was then (by a large margin) the most admired company in the world. I was a frequent visitor to IBM corporate headquarters in Armonk, New York. On most workdays someone could fire a cannonball down the halls of corporate headquarters at 5:15 P.M. and hit no one. Even the professional and managerial employees worked 35 to 45 hours per week, took time off when they had minor health problems, and enjoyed five weeks of real vacation—with no cell phones or personal computers. They took comfort in the belief that they could look forward to a lifetime of guaranteed job security.

Those days—and those jobs—seem like a distant dream. Today the employees in that same building work 60 to 80 hours per week, keep on working through most health problems, and take almost no real vacation. They are not counting on any guaranteed job security.

This year I was developing an executive education seminar for one of the world's most successful banks. I asked the coordinator of the session, "How many hours a week does the average executive in this program work?" His very sober answer was "Over 80!"

This book is written for leaders—and for professionals who aspire to be leaders. For both professionals and leaders the entire world of work has changed. Global competition, new technology, massive economic problems, and job insecurity have been factors in the creation of a new world of work. This new world of professional work is more challenging than at any time in my life.

If you are working 35 to 45 hours per week and take five weeks of real vacation, work-life balance may not be a huge issue. If you are working more than 50 hours per week and get almost no real vacation, then work-life balance has a very different meaning. For today's professionals, if life is somehow disconnected from work, lots of us won't have very meaningful lives.

This book would have been very important in 1979. This book is critically important today. It was needed then. It is really needed now!

In many developed countries, employee engagement is at an all-time low. It is past time for a turn-around.

I know of no couple who can address the *why* of work better than Dave and Wendy Ulrich. Dave is one of the world's great business thinkers. I respect his work more than anyone in his field. Dave is an expert in understanding how organizations are impacted by individuals. Wendy Ulrich represents the "micro" to Dave's "macro." Wendy is a wonderful psychologist who deeply understands how individuals are impacted by organizations. Along with being great thinkers and professionals, Dave and Wendy are great human beings. They truly care about the organizations and people that they touch. They are dedicated to helping leaders created more effective organizations and helping human beings have more fulfilling lives. They wrote this book because they want to help you, the reader, and your organization achieve more abundance.

Peter Drucker once told me, "The leader of the past knew how to tell. The leader of the future will know how to ask." Today's leaders and professionals continually interact with knowledge workers. Peter taught us that knowledge workers are any employees who know more about what they are doing than we do. I guess that if we knew more about what was going on in other professional's work than they did, we could just tell them what to do and how to do it. In today's complex world, no leader or employee knows more than the knowledgeable professionals that surround us. We all have to ask for other people's ideas, listen, and learn.

Dave and Wendy have followed Peter Drucker's lead and organized this book around the asking of seven wonderful questions. By asking these questions—to ourselves and the members of our teams—listening to the responses and learning, we can create a more abundant world of work for both companies and the individuals who populate these companies.

The answers to the seven questions in *The Way of Work* will help you and your organization: develop a positive identity, gain real commitment, build positive relationships, create a great environment, find deeper meaning, achieve continuous learning, and experience true happiness. What can be more important than that?

I want to end this Foreword with a challenge. Don't just read this book as a dispassionate observer; apply what you learn in each chapter to yourself and to your organization. Use these seven questions as a mirror to help you understand yourself and your organization.

The world will not become a better place because we learn—the world will only become a better place when we do.

What is the why in the work behind *The Why of Work?* Dave and Wendy Ulrich have years of invaluable experience in individual and organizational advising, research, study, and reflection. *The Why of Work* is a wonderful synthesis of their years of learning. I can say without doubt that my life is better and more abundant because I have learned from Dave and Wendy. This book is intended to help you and your organization have a better and more abundant life.

Read *The Why of Work*—and then do something that is much more important—do the work that is needed to help yourself, the people you love, and your organization have a better and more abundant life!

—Marshall Goldsmith is the author of the *New York Times* and international bestsellers *Mojo* and *What Got You Here Won't Get You There*, the Harold Longman Award winner for Business Book of the Year. He lives in Rancho Santa Fe, California, and New York City.

PREFACE

This book evolved out of a conversation between a business professor/consultant (Dave) and a psychologist (Wendy), a conversation that has seasoned more than 10 years of morning walks along the riverways of Michigan, the neighborhoods of Quebec, and the mountain trails of Utah. For more reasons than one, this conversation often leaves us breathless as we contemplate the challenges faced by leaders who create the organizations we respectively encounter. Theirs are the challenges we face as well: finding the *why* to sustain the *how* of our daily living. This book focuses on a simple question: How do great leaders create, for themselves and others, a sense of abundance (meaning, purpose, hope, pleasure) that not only engages employees but also delivers value to customers, investors, and communities?

Dave works to help organizations create value for employees, customers, investors, and communities. He coaches leaders on how to build corporate agendas, organizational capabilities, and the human resource infrastructures to achieve their goals and objectives Dave is also trained as a taxonomist who looks for simple patterns in complex phenomena. In these pursuits, Dave sometimes encounters leaders who formulate great strategies, structures, and processes but may overlook the heart and soul that make organizations meaningful places to work.

Wendy works to help people change and heal. With a background in psychodynamic, cognitive, and family therapy as well as positive psychology, she helps clients examine the patterns that have shaped their past so they can better choose their future. Her clinical practice and change workshops include both people with everyday struggles and people facing trauma or serious adversity. Some people in each group see primarily the senselessness and deficits of their lives, while others manage to find a sense of meaning and abundance. Her M.B.A. reminds her that real change means institutionalizing, not merely individualizing, abundance and meaning.

One of us works with organizations, the other with individuals. One wants to help organizations serve their customers and investors; the other wants to help individuals grow and find peace. But as we have worked together, we have found common ground. The questions both leaders and those they lead wrestle with and the answers they develop seem to overlap and connect around the search for *The Why of Work*—the search for meaning, purpose. Finding that *why* infuses organizations with a sense of abundance—having enough and to spare of what matters most.

Dave had a personal encounter with abundance a few years ago while we shared responsibilities directing a mission for our church in Canada. One day he met with a poor African immigrant family living in subsidized housing with shoddy furniture and too many people for the confined space. Despite these "deficits," this family had forged an emotional bond that emanated warmth and generosity. They cared about each other and the world. They were curious and compassionate. When it came to what mattered most, they had enough and to spare. Later that day, we had dinner in an executive's expensive, beautifully adorned home. Although the food was tasty and the furnishings elegant, the conversation and preoccupations of the evening were superficial and sterile. We both learned once again that meaning is tied less to belongings and more to emotional bonds, a sense of purpose, and using one's skills to serve the needs of others.

In organizations as well, meaning and abundance are more about what we do with what we have than about what we have to begin with or what we accumulate. They are more about finding the resources to deal with our challenges than about having unlimited resources to make work easy or effortless. Work will always be work—sometimes monotonous or routine, sometimes stressful to the max—but we believe work can still contribute more than just money to our lives. Leaders can develop the resources to make employees work harder and to make work work for employees. There is a strong business case for helping people find meaning at work. As employees find meaning, they contribute to the broadest purposes for which organizations exist: creating value for customers, investors, and communities. This book distills from a broad range of literature and research a set of resources leaders can use in that process.

As we have worked with college students and young missionaries, we have been infected with the rising generation's passion for purpose around both ideas and ideals. As we have worked with mature adults, we have learned that meaning seekers abound at all life stages. We have seen that people find meaning not only in their personal lives but also through the organizations where they learn, worship, socialize, and play. Meaning can be discovered in friendships, families, neighborhoods, religious communities, schools, service clubs . . . and work.

On a more personal level, we seem to be constantly asking ourselves, "What will we do when we grow up?" When younger we assumed this question would be well resolved by the time we were 30, but it has lingered into our children's 30s. Is meaning found in taking vacations, learning, giving, serving our neighbors, or building a business? The answer can be yes to each of these. And it can also be no. People find meaning in many places and activities, but for us and many we know, meaning itself is not optional. It is the object of a nearly universal search. Work is a nearly universal setting for engaging in this quest.

The problems we face as a consultant and a psychologist, the experiences we have had through serving others, and our personal meaning journey have occupied our thinking for a long time. As we tried to figure out what meaning means, why it matters, and how to develop it, we realized we had embarked on a complicated journey. Wendy has taught and supervised psychology graduate students, run workshops on personal abundance, consulted for a variety of organizations, and written books on forgiving ourselves and changing our mind-set. Dave has coached and trained countless executives and HR professionals on how to diagnose and build organizational capabilities and deliver value to customers, writing more than 20 books on these topics. In each of these forums, we interviewed people to find out how they interpret the sources of potential meaning in their lives. We asked flight attendants, janitorial workers, bus drivers, homemakers, and executives what they liked about their jobs and what gave meaning to their personal and professional lives. We looked for underlying patterns of individual and organizational meaning and success. We also went to our respective literatures for research and theory on meaning and living well. Many thoughtful people in many fields of inquiry have studied different aspects of how meaning and personal well-being are defined, experienced, and developed.

In the spirit of taxonomy, we culled our experience, our conversations, and the theory and research that informed our work and identified seven disciplines, each of which looks at meaning making through a slightly different lens: positive psychology, social responsibility, marriage and interpersonal relationships (including high-performing teams), employee engagement, culture and positive work environment, growth and learning, and happiness. The ideas and research from each of these disciplines contribute to the model driving this book: seven drivers, questions, and tool sets that leaders may use to build meaning, in turn creating a strong organizational purpose and identity that create value for customers, investors, and employees alike.

Two caveats are in order. First, we know we have not done justice to any of the disciplines we synthesize. Volumes of theory and research discuss positive psychology, social responsibility, marriage and interpersonal relationships (including high-performing teams), employee engagement, culture and positive work environment, growth and learning, and happiness. We have tried to pare down these vast literatures into a set of manageable tasks for leaders who want to help employees find meaning in their professional lives. Second, we realize we are writing about very personal issues within a professional setting. Consistent with that agenda, we have used a lot of personal stories to illustrate how to define and determine meaning. By personalizing meaning, we hope we can capture why and how leaders make meaning happen, build abundant organizations, and deliver value to stakeholders.

This brings us to the issue of the audience for this book: leaders. Whether talking to executives of global companies or therapy clients who struggle with loss and grief, we have found the search for meaning to be universal. It affects rich and poor; young and old; American, African, European, and Asian; those in big and small organizations, publicly traded firms and public agencies; employees close to retirement and employees just entering the workforce; those who volunteer in community organizations and those who lead large conglomerates; those who are unemployed and those who put in 80-hour weeks. Given our professional interests, we could have written to individuals at large, to employees, or to HR professionals (who generally accept the importance of meaning making and who build HR systems to sustain it). We decided to write to leaders.

Leaders are meaning makers: they set direction that others aspire to; they help others participate in doing good work and good works; they communicate ideas and invest in practices that shape how people think, act, and feel. As organizations become an increasing part of the individual's sense of identity and purpose, leaders play an increasing role in helping people shape the meaning of their lives. Too many leaders focus on where they are going and how to get there, without paying much attention to how it feels to those on the journey with them. When leaders make work meaningful, they help create abundant organizations where employees operate on a value proposition based on meaning as well as money. Meaning becomes a multiplier of employee competence and commitment, a lead indicator of customer share, a source of investor confidence, and a factor in ensuring social responsibility in the broader community. We find that even the hardest-nosed leaders become interested in meaning when they realize its potential contribution to bottom-line realities. When leaders grasp the why of meaning, they then seek the how.

Our Meaning Makers

We pay tribute to those who have helped us experience, think about, and attempt to understand and deliver meaning. We have each lost our father in recent months. To them we owe great gratitude for the lessons they taught by example and word. Our mothers continue to find meaning and enlarge it for others as their abilities allow, and they along with our wonderful siblings (Belinda, Carla, and Eric) and their families are models of grace, charity, humor, and hope. They have built abundant worlds for us, and we hope to pass that legacy to our children and theirs. We consider our children among our best colleagues, thought stimulators, and most abundant abundance enhancers: Carrie Kelley, Monika Ulrich, and Mike Ulrich, with his wife, Melanie Swenson Ulrich, and our sweet granddaughter, Maren. We dedicate this book to her as our tangible symbol of hope for our future and the world's future.

We have professional colleagues who are close friends whose ideas and care support and sustain us. The list is long, but we are grateful to insights and input from (in alphabetical order) the Alpine 6th Ward, Loretta Allen, Dick Beatty, Allen Bergin, Ginger Bitter, Karen Blake, Wayne and Nancy Brockbank, Kim Cameron, Ralph Christensen, Bob Eichinger, Kathleen Flake, Rich Ferre, Jac Fitz-enz, Marshall Goldsmith, Lynda Gratton, Michelle Holt, Bill Joyce, Steve Kerr, Dave Klimek, Dale and Gerry Lake, Ed

Lawler, Mike Losey, Paul McKinnon, Susan Meisinger, Henry Mintzberg, Chris Packard, Jeffrey Pfeffer, CK Prahalad, Scott Richards, Bonner Ritchie, Libby Sartain, Judy Seegmiller, Norm Smallwood, Kate Sweetman, and Jon Younger. We owe a special thanks to Danny Stern, who advised us as a friend and agent. This book would not have come to fruition without the skillful shepherding of Mary Glenn and her staff at McGraw-Hill.

We are also indebted to professional colleagues who have written about these subjects with enormous insight and whose ideas inform our thinking: Viktor Frankl, whose marvelous book captures the search for meaning in impossible circumstances; Judy Bardwick, who has been so insightful at capturing many of these insights; Lynda Gratton, who brings a keen and kind eye to helping people find purpose at work; Kenneth Moore, who has the ability to bring spiritual insights into the work setting; Martin Seligman and his colleagues, who have shaped the field of positive psychology; and individuals such as Jacques Lusseyran, Teeda Butt Mam, Imaculee Ilibagiza, and Joseph Smith, whose stories of meaning making in the face of the most meaning-robbing forms of human suffering have encouraged us to believe that meaning making is not only always possible but also imperative.

We also thank our professional colleagues at the RBL Group (rbl.net) and Sixteen Stones Center for Growth (six teenstones.net), who touch our lives as both thought partners and advisers. We are most grateful to participants in workshops and retreats who have shared their stories, insights, and honest hopes for the future.

So, Why Have We Written This Book?

We have written this book because we hope to synthesize and simplify mystical and complex approaches to meaning into focused questions and specific actions.

We hope to further a serious discussion of the nature of personal meaning at work.

We hope to show leaders that attention to meaning will help them reach their financial, customer, organizational, community, and strategic goals.

We hope to offer leaders specific ideas, tools, and practices for growing meaning and abundance.

We hope to redefine leaders' roles to include not only direction setting and structure providing but meaning making as well.

We hope to promote for all of us who go to work day in and day out a sense of greater abundance because we have a clearer sense of the meaning of our labor.

We hope to change the conversations between leaders and employees to focus not only on what needs to be done but also on how it feels to do it.

We hope to turn deficit-laden thinking into abundance metaphors and actions that will make a better world for our children, their children, and yours. For more information about this book, visit our website: thewhyofwork.com.

—Dave and Wendy Ulrich
Alpine, Utah

CHAPTER 1

The Case for Meaning

This morning, people all over the planet got out of bed and got ready for work. Some headed out before dawn in high-end cars to claim high-rise offices with high-tech computers and highbrow clients. Some headed out before dawn to walk barefoot, wares on their head, to claim a choice spot in the dirt near the entrance to the village market. Some wrestled with the muses to create artistic masterpieces or solve perplexing scientific problems. Others wrestled with boredom to complete their shifts at cash registers, call centers, or assembly lines. Some pitched their résumés in business suits, looking for good benefits and a sure path to comfortable retirement. Some made their pitch in ragged jeans on street corners, looking for someone to rent their muscles for at least the day.

Some people in each one of these and many other categories by which we could define work found a sense of meaning, purpose, even abundance in their labor today. Others in each category found world-weary tedium, frustration, and despair.

Which were you?

Which were the people you lead?

Viktor Frankl was a budding psychologist following in the footsteps of Freud when World War II erupted. Frankl survived three years in a Nazi concentration camp, but upon his liberation he found his family, home, and writings gone. Before the war Frankl had been developing a system of psychotherapy based on our need for meaning. Once he was incarcerated, his previous philosophical speculations about what helps people heal and cope were no longer just interesting cerebral playthings; they were tested in the fire of a dreadful and lengthy ordeal. Frankl's book *Man's Search for Meaning,* which has sold more than nine million copies, has become a classic. Against the backdrop of horrific adversity, his insistence on the possibility—even the necessity—of finding meaning in life becomes deeply credible. After all, adversity generally disrupts our sense of meaning and robs life of what previously gave it sense and purpose. In troubled times our search for meaning becomes both more difficult and more compelling. Frankl quotes the philosopher Friedrich Nietzsche: "He who has a *why* to live can bear with almost any *how.*"

He or she who has a *why to work* can bear with almost any how as well. Obviously, people find meaning in many settings—in the privacy of homes and the expanses of nature, in churches, ballparks, and community centers, in family and friendship circles. But work takes the lion's share of our time and energy. Most of us spend more time at work than at play, at family gatherings, at religious meetings, or at hobbies. The organizations in which we labor are thus a primary setting not only for accomplishing assignments but also for finding an abiding sense of meaning in life. Work is a universal setting in which to pursue our universal search for meaning.

Meaning at Work

This book is about both the *why* and the *how* of meaning at work.

The *why* refers to the human search for meaning that finds its way into our offices and factories, a search that motivates, inspires, and defines us. The *how* gets us into the practicalities of how leaders facilitate that search personally and among their employees. We offer many specific tools and principles to help leaders put meaning to work not only to build personal meaning but also to help companies succeed in the marketplace of human endeavor.

Thus the search for meaning adds value in two senses of the word. First, humans are meaning-making machines who find *inherent value* in making sense out of life. The meaning we make of an experience determines its impact on us and can turn disaster into opportunity, loss into hope, failure into learning, boredom into reflection. The meaning we create can make life feel rich and full regardless of our external circumstances or give us the courage to change our external circumstances. When we find meaning in our work, we find meaning in life.

In addition to inherent value, meaning has *market value*. Meaningful work solves real problems, contributes real benefits, and thus adds real value to customers and investors. Employees who find meaning in their work are more satisfied, more engaged, and in turn more productive. They work harder, smarter, more passionately and creatively. They learn and adapt. They are more connected to customer needs. And they stick around. Leaders invest in meaning making not only because it is noble but also because it is profitable. Making sense can also make cents.

The Abundant Organization

In this book we refer to companies that are meaningful in both of these senses of the word as *abundant organizations.* An abundant organization *is a work setting in which individuals coordinate their aspirations and actions to create meaning for themselves, value for stakeholders, and hope for humanity at large.* An abundant organization is one that has *enough and to spare of the things that matter most*: creativity, hope, resilience, determination, resourcefulness, and leadership.

Abundant organizations are profitable organizations, but rather than focusing only on assumptions of competition and scarcity, abundant organizations also focus on opportunity and synergy. Rather than accepting the fear-based breakdown of meaning in hard times, abundant organizations concentrate on bringing order, integrity, and purpose out of chaos and disintegration. Rather than restricting themselves to narrow, self-serving agendas, abundant organizations integrate a diversity of human needs, experiences, and timetables.

In good times and in hard times, abundant organizations create meaning for both the employees who comprise them and the customers who keep them in business. Employees, customers, investors, and society benefit when employees find meaning at work and when companies give meaning to society. This logic applies to small and large organizations, to public agencies and private enterprises, to local storefronts and global conglomerates.

The Market Value of Why

Even if you are not one of those rare folks blessed with a gift for finding joy in the concentration camps of life, you intuitively know that you and your work team would be more productive, more satisfied, and more creative if work engaged not only your head and your hands but your heart and soul as well. What most of us know intuitively research confirms: when employees find meaning at work, they care enough about it to develop their competence; they work harder and are more productive; they stay longer and are more positive about their work experience. But there is more: when employees are more positive, customers generally respond in kind. Employee attitude is a key lead indicator of customer attitude, and satisfied customers help the businesses they patronize to survive and thrive. In brief:

1. Employees who find meaning at work are more competent, committed, and contributing.
2. In turn, employee competence, commitment, and sense of contribution lead to increased customer commitment.
3. In turn, customer commitment leads to better financial results for the company.

Making meaning is an important cause and a lead indicator of long-term organizational success. So-called intangibles explain about 50 percent of the market value of publicly traded firms.[1] Intangibles are the assets and capabilities of a company that cannot be touched or put on a balance sheet but give investors confidence in the future earnings of the company. Intangibles include nonthings such as leadership, talent, innovation, skill, and vision. Investors increasingly value these intangible organizational capabilities because they increase confidence in a company's future success.

Employee competence, commitment, and passion or energy are among these intangible assets. Employees can

5

be competent, even committed, but still lack passion for their work. Meaning reinforces employees' passion for work because it ties what they do to a greater good that also pays off in the marketplace. Passion for work is an intangible asset that has a direct impact on a firm's market value.

Consider some additional data points on the value for both employees and customers of abundant organizations (exemplified here in organizations that employees like to work for, that investors admire, that invest in people, and that have positive work practices):

- Over a 10-year period (1998 to 2008) "best companies to work for" have a 6.8 percent stock appreciation versus 1.0 percent for the average firm.
- Over a seven-year period, the most-admired firms in *Fortune*'s list of admired companies had doubled the market returns of competitors.
- The probability of an initial public offering (IPO; a new company) succeeding goes from 60 to 79 percent when the new company invests in its people.
- Sixty-one hospitals in the United Kingdom had a 7 percent decline in death rate when they invested in the well-being of their staff.
- A one-standard-deviation increase in high-performance work practices yields $27,044 increase in sales per employee and $3,814 increase in profit per employee.
- Only 13 percent of disengaged employees would recommend their company's products or services, compared with 78 percent of engaged employees.
- Disengaged employees are 10 times more likely to say they will leave their company within a year.

Franklin D. Roosevelt, U.S. president during the Great Depression of the 1930s, said, "We have always known that heedless self-interest was bad morals. We know now that it is bad economics." This is even more true in today's transparent and fluid cultures.

Leaders as Meaning Makers

So, how are abundant organizations created? This is the task of leadership.

Ultimately the crisis of meaning is always a crisis of leadership. We hope to structure for leaders the private conversations and corporate decision-making criteria that shape abundant organizations. Abundance is not only a prerogative for leaders of rich people, smart people, prestigious people, successful people. Meaning is not only in short supply for poor people, mediocre people, struggling people, hurting people. Great leaders recognize the vital importance of abundance and meaning to everyone in their organization. Including themselves.

The Great Place to Work Institute has conducted surveys of the best companies to work for in America since 1980. It now does work in more than 30 countries. Its surveys serve as a confirmation of the impact of *The Why of Work* on business results. A portfolio consisting of all of the publicly traded companies on the Best Companies to Work For list each year from 1998 to 2008 would have earned an annual return of 6.80 percent, compared to just 1.04 percent over the same period for the Standard & Poor's 500. Even purchasing stock in companies on the list in 1998 and holding it for the ensuing 10 years would have achieved a return of 4.15 percent, which is also much higher than the comparable indices.

What do these companies do to maintain this outstanding performance? Of course they make money via excellent customer service and many other solid management practices or they would not survive. But in addition these high performers tap into the elusive quality of meaning in a variety of ways. For example, in the last 25 years, five companies have consistently been highly rated: Goldman Sachs, Nordstrom, Publix Super Markets, REI, and W. L. Gore & Associates.[2] Goldman leaders build a culture of "smart people working together," or one of collaboration and synergy. Nordstrom has earned a reputation for exceptional customer service, hiring employees who delight in "anticipating and meeting customer needs." Publix Super Markets, founded in 1930, also has a strong customer focus, cultivating "servant leaders" who treat "associates" (not "employees") with respect and who become active in their communities. REI (a recreational equipment cooperative) trains leaders to build cooperation among employees and between employees and customers to accomplish its mission of "inspiring, educating, and outfitting for a lifetime of outdoor adventure and stewardship." Gore & Associates leaders encourage employees to pursue innovation by living by a set of guiding principles of "freedom, fairness, commitment, and waterline." In each of these exceptional companies, leaders endeavor to turn the meaning employees find in their work into sustained organizational abundance. Though each company has a unique take on how to make this connection, all develop leaders who help employees find meaning at work that contributes to organizational success.

The creation of meaning applies to countries as well as companies. Bhutan is a small country located in the Himalaya Mountains in South Asia. Although most countries use the Gross National Product index to measure national success, in 1972 King Jigme Singye Wangchuck of Bhutan instituted a Gross National Happiness (GNH) index to assess his country's progress. The king instituted social and economic policies to help Bhutan citizens find meaning and well-being in their lives. The GNH index includes measures of the progress of sustainable development, preservation of cultural values, conservation of the natural environment, and establishment of good governance. Even with low gross domestic product per capita, Bhutan citizens are among the happiest in the world, with over 50 percent of citizens reporting they are "very happy." Their lifespan is in the top 10 percent of nations worldwide. Bhutan became the world's newest democracy in 2008 as the king established parliamentary elections, Jigmi Thinley, the first Bhutan prime minister, has said, "material enrichment and consumerist ethics must not lead to spiritual impoverishment. True happiness and well-being lies in sustainable education, health, and living environments which include caring and sharing relationships where extended families serve each other."[3]

In companies or in countries, leaders have the task of creating a direction for their organizations that is charged with meaning—that resonates with not only the minds and hands but the hearts of those they lead. In this book, we go beyond cases to synthesize and integrate theory, research, and experience from multiple disciplines to propose seven meaning drivers successful leaders have used to shape meaning. An individual leader might be predisposed to focus on one or two elements of an abundant organization, as shown in the preceding examples. We cull these and many other examples to offer leaders a menu of questions and activities to help them create meaning for employees and turn it into sustained organizational abundance.

Recessions of Meaning

In either good or bad markets, without bottom-line results organizations will simply fold, leaving even able workers twiddling their thumbs. Organizations in any economy must also make sense to the people who compose them. When our organizations enact our highest values and embody our best aspirations, they inspire our best efforts, and nothing short of our best efforts will keep us afloat when storms are raging and the ship has sprung a leak—*or* when fair winds lull us into lethargy and hubris.

In the 2009 recession, many governments bailed out companies with toxic assets. Bailing out sinking ships is a bad analogy for what makes organizations seaworthy, however. Before setting out for open seas, we must not only bail out the water but fix the leaks. Organization leaks occur not only when leaders fail to provide great products and solid returns, but also when they waver on ethical principles, isolate themselves from the consequences of their choices, abdicate responsibilities for strategy and innovation, or drop the ball of timely action. Organization leaks also occur when employees put in their time but don't invest their hearts, when they abandon creativity or integrity, or when they lose sight of the impact of their work. Organizations that survive in recessions and thrive during recovery will have leaders who consistently offer employees both economic well-being and an abundance of meaning and purpose.

In both lean and prosperous times, an organization's values are tested and forged, setting the stage for the future. Meaning is shaped or dissipated. Loyalties are won or lost. Talent and skill are honed or abandoned. Creativity and problem-solving skill are developed or undermined. And future sustainability is either ensured or threatened.

We need abundant organizations in deficit-dominated contexts that challenge our existing sense of meaning and growth-dominated contexts that give rise to expansion.

Even when the world economy improves, the ghosts of our "psychological recession"[4] haunt us. Financial challenges are embedded in larger trends that permeate society. In downturns people feel an increasing sense of malaise, anomie, and isolation that robs them of meaning and direction. Crises in financial markets echo the crises in personal lives and social movements—crises that, almost by definition, undercut our ability to make sense of our lives and figure out what to do next. Crises sabotage the daily routines that have grown out of our values, beliefs, and past experience. Crises threaten the assumptions that we hold without even realizing it about what life means in both good times and in bad. In brief, crises increase our sense of malaise, anomie, isolation, or deficit, robbing us all of meaning and hope.

Frankl's *why* and *how* questions about meaning apply in both bad and good markets, at work and at home, in domestic settings as well as in organizations that span the globe. Good times can temporarily distract us from such questions, but the questions always come back around. As Frankl suggests, the search for meaning is more about how we think than about the circumstances in which we find ourselves. Deficit thinking can abound even in the midst of plenty.

The Prevalence of Deficit Thinking

Have you ever been robbed? Our friend Rena's home was broken into. A small home safe containing her family heirlooms and personal papers was taken, along with some money, a computer, and jewelry. Rena is not a wealthy person. What was taken had relatively little economic value, but it included much that brought to her life a sense of meaning, identity, and connection with her past—a letter for her adopted son from his birth mother, Rena's father's World War II medals, a personal journal, a stack of prized letters from her mother, her grandmother's antique music box, the ring of a deceased friend. Rena lost her sense that she lived in a safe community, that her home was a haven, that a benevolent presence was protecting her family. As we can easily imagine, Rena became more skittish and vigilant, more protective of her children, more interested in home security ads on TV. Doors were locked more consistently. Sleep was interrupted by nightmares. Rena wished she could create an impenetrable wall to lock up her home, her family, her heart.

Like Rena, when employees lose what they have come to count on and expect—be it a person, an income, a position, or less concrete notions like security, identity, or direction— they are inclined to deficit thinking, a common problem when people stand to lose not only their personal treasures but also their retirement, their colleagues, their jobs. Deficit thinking is probably inevitable, perhaps even helpful, in some situations, but when leaders' thinking is dominated by an agenda of self-protection, deficit thinking itself becomes the burglar. Deficit thinking can lock us into a prison of our own making, a prison dominated by fear, isolation, disorientation, and competition for scarce resources. Even if we get back what we lost—even if the economy improves, the takeover is averted, or we end up with a better job than before—our deficit thinking can continue to cast a discomfiting spell over our lives.

The world of deficit thinking pervades both personal and organizational life. The thieves and robbers of crisis undermine the ability of leaders to foster abundance. Of course, economic hardships, political uncertainties, family disruptions, illness, death, and even horrific suffering are hardly new kids on humanity's block. Grim realities have always inhabited our collective neighborhoods. It is still quite another matter when they move into our basement, our spare room, even our master suite. Once we realize the precariousness of the things we have come to depend on for security, security cannot be restored fully until our dependencies change. This is where great leaders come in.

At about age three, children in every culture begin badgering their parents with the question "Why?" The search for meaning begins early, but youthful philosophies that comfortably accommodated the distant existence of Trouble may require reevaluation when Trouble becomes our bed partner. Trouble may be as simple as a changed corporate policy or as complicated as a bankruptcy, as removed as an unhappy customer 3,000 miles away or as personal as losing a child. Leaders must refine and redefine their own answers to "Why?" and must help others do so as well. They must tackle not only the meaning of suffering but also the meaning of prosperity, opportunity, or just another day knocking on doors. When we need to solve complex problems, preserve the bottom line, and maintain motivation to try again, the search for meaning moves out of the domain of philosophers and theologians and finds its way to the top of the to-do lists of hard-minded corporate leaders.

Leaders spearhead the search for meaning in both good times and bad. In up markets, when talent is scarce, meaning matters because employees are essentially volunteers who can choose where to allocate their time and energy. In recessions, employee engagement or satisfaction scores would be expected to fall with the market; however, many organizations see false positives on such surveys because of a gratitude effect (employees compare themselves with their less fortunate colleagues or friends and are grateful to have any job at all, even if it is not especially meaningful). Either way, memories last longer than recessions. Employees who felt mistreated during a down market or whose meaning at work is found only in crisis containment are more likely to leave when things settle down and they have more options.

Consider the following cases of employees and leaders in different types of companies and at different career stages:

o **Personal insecurities.** Vicki, a young professional with college diploma in hand, felt extremely lucky to win an ideal job at a top-brand company. She worked hard on assigned tasks and skillfully negotiated the daily politics of the office. But during a serious economic downturn her firm initiated first one and then a second and third round of layoffs in a matter of months. At first only lower-performing people were let go; then even talented, senior people were cut loose to face the shrinking job market. The atmosphere at the office turned from collegial to cynical and from cooperative to competitive. Vicki worked even longer hours to keep her job, and she worried incessantly about her future. The demands at work kept her away from hobbies and friends, invaded her relationship with her husband, and touched off old problems with depression and anxiety. The rhythms and routines of her life began to feel jagged and contorted almost beyond recognition, and all her stories became tinged with fear.

o **Work/life balance.** Raj is a successful Indian entrepreneur, proud of the company he has built. The company he started 12 years ago has grown to more than 80 employees, with a strong brand and customer loyalty. But he knows that to go the next step of continued growth he will have to invest in becoming more global and even more innovative. This will require both personal energy and more time traveling in North America, Europe, and Asia, the most likely prospects for his company. With teenage children who are both happy to see him home and sometimes happy to see him gone, Raj knows he would pay a large personal price for the next phase of company growth. He debates whether he has the energy to do what it would take to move his company forward or should coast on previous successes for a while.

o **Undermined security and flexibility.** Grant and Shirlyn have worked hard their entire professional lives. Grant started with his current company 25 years ago, right out of college. Shirlyn did substitute teaching until her children were older; then she began teaching full-time. They had hoped that when their last child left for college they would have more opportunities to travel and develop hobbies. Although Grant feels reasonably secure in his job, changing market conditions have led him to lay off 25 percent of his employees. Those who remain have to do not only their work but also the work of those who left. People are nervous about their jobs and frustrated about longer work hours. School budget squeezes have also led to increased class sizes and more stress for Shirlyn. Grant's and Shirlyn's retirement savings have been reduced about 20 percent in the declining stock market, and they will have to work for another three or four years to recover. Work has become drudgery as they face these unanticipated realities. But work also forestalls the necessary question: what will give meaning to my life when I retire?

○ **The liability of success.** Ivan was the successful one. In school he got the top grades, was popular, and was targeted as a future leader. At work he moved up quickly, becoming not only wealthy but powerful. He paid a personal price with two divorces and alienated children, but he hoped his kids would come back around as they matured. He savored the daily challenges of his work and put his mind and heart into it. Gradually, however, Ivan began to feel disconnected from the heart of his work. Sitting in his luxurious office, he realized it had been a long time since he had interacted directly with the customers who used to make him feel good about his company. He had not really visited employees on the front line in years, and when he met with them in formal meetings they seemed aloof. Those closest to him continued to tell him how talented and successful he was, and he was surrounded by all the trappings of success. But he started to wonder if he had lost touch with what he really loved. He saw himself resembling the Dickens character Scrooge more with each passing day.

Most of us as leaders have been or have had such employees in our organizations. Many of us have personally experienced both economic malaise and the pitfalls of success, either first-hand or among our families and friends. Unfortunately, these cases are not isolated; they represent developing patterns in today's world. Without overfocusing on depressing realities, leaders will recognize something of the depth and breadth of this malaise. Skim the following for a quick overview of some of these trends.

1. **Declining mental health and happiness.** Building on the work initiated in Bhutan, the New Economics Foundation, which has calculated happiness scores for 178 countries, concludes that most countries of the world face a crisis of unhappiness.[5] More specifically, statistics on personal well-being indicate increases in clinical depression, anxiety, and addiction. Eight to 10 percent of Americans over age 18 suffer from some depressive disorder, while in developing countries depression affects 15 percent of the population with 80 percent of those afflicted untreated.[6] Anxiety disorders (including panic disorder, obsessive-compulsive disorder, posttraumatic stress disorder, and social phobia) covary with depression, and about 18 percent of U.S. citizens face one of these anxiety challenges in a given year.[7] Addiction disorders (including eating disorders and substance abuse) are also on the rise.[8] Mental health disorders are the leading cause of disability in the United States for people aged

15 to 44, directly and indirectly affecting employee costs. People seem to be losing touch with their strengths as more lives are dominated by weaknesses with a focus on what is wrong.

2. **Increased concern for environmental demands, social responsibility, organization purpose, and individual motivation.** Scholars estimate that humans currently consume 30 percent more resources than the earth can produce.[9] Between 1961 and 2006, human demand on the biosphere more than doubled. These demands threaten habitats, air quality, and climate stability. For example, between 1961 and 2001, the consumption of fossil fuels (coal, oil, gas) increased by almost 700 percent. At present rates of consumption, we could run out of these fuels in the next 25 years.[10] In part because of their poor handling of environmental concerns, many social institutions face waning stakeholder respect. Institutional cynicism runs high in political, business, educational, and religious settings. People distrust organizations they believe do little to protect the earth or serve its poorest inhabitants.[11] More than three-quarters (79 percent) of the world's most admired companies have seen their reputation decline in recent years.[12] Eroding corporate reputation, increased institutional cynicism, and poor records on environmental responsibility underlie this loss, alienating many high-potential employees.

3. **Increased complexity of work.** Technology, globalization, and demographics all add to the complexity of the workplace. With technological advances, the half-life of knowledge has shortened. The Internet has newly become the standard source of information, with 60

percent of Internet users online daily and 70 percent of businesses having a website.[13] Customers have more information and choice than ever about what and how to buy, and distant markets have replaced local markets in many industries.[14] Global companies have 24-hour operations among their locations around the world. Workforce demographics are becoming increasingly diversified around race, ethnicity,[15] social class, gender, sexual orientation, age, religion, and nationality.[16] Corporations face the major challenge of how to respect and make good use of these differences in increasingly diverse workforces. For example, as GenMe or Generation Y employees (born between 1981 and 1999) move into the workforce, their values (like self-esteem, self-interest, and leisure time[17]) often clash with those of the baby-boom generation,[18] creating the need for policies and practices that appeal to and motivate various subgroups. All of these technological, global, and demographic trends make work more complex, necessitating both more specialization and more teamwork to respond. Teamwork requires unprecedented skill in cooperation, prioritization, and communication—skills often underdeveloped in an age of text messaging rather than in-person relating.

4. **Increased isolation.** Proliferating electronics, high mobility, and urban sprawl have all been blamed for increased social isolation. Those who spend hours in front of a computer screen spend less time with real people, Wiki and chat groups notwithstanding. U.S. households own an average of 2.24 televisions, with each television running for an average of 6 hours and 47 minutes per day and the average child watching TV

1,680 minutes per week (28 hours a week; 4 hours a day).[19] Fewer Americans participate in civic movements like signing petitions, voting, or attending club meetings, and entertaining at home is half as common now as 20 years ago.[20] The sense of isolation spreads to the workplace as job changes, international assignments, and constantly shifting work groups dominate the work landscape and undermine the sense of community. People lose the stories, the history, the heroes, and the routines of small interactions that form the bonds of connection. In a work setting, countering these trends means building a culture and work setting that unite and unify people.

5. **Low employee commitment.** A recent analysis of data by HR Solutions, Inc., found that an astonishing 50 percent of employees said yes when asked if they had thought of resigning in the last six months. According to a Saratoga Institute study of more than 19,000 U.S. workers in 17 industries, 72 percent of employees who quit leave because they feel they are not being recognized for their contributions or sufficiently respected and coached by their leaders.[21] *Gallup Management Journal's* semiannual Employee Engagement Index shows that only 29 percent of employees are actively engaged in their jobs, while 54 percent are not engaged and 17 percent are actively disengaged.[22] Right Management (a consulting firm) found similar results with only 34 percent of employees fully engaged while 50 percent are completely disengaged. Nine percent are engaged by their organization but not their job, and 7 percent are engaged by their job but not the organization.[23] The cost of lost productivity in the United States is estimated to be between $287

and $370 billion.[24] In the United Kingdom, research from YouGov on more than 40,000 employees reports that only half (51 percent) of employees feel fully engaged by their company.[25] Disengaged employees are less likely to meet corporate goals or to stay with the firm.[26] When only fear of unemployment keeps employees on the job, they are probably not giving their best.

6. **Growing disposability and change.** We live in a world of increasingly disposable products—from diapers to pens to shoes to electronic devices. Instead of repairing and reusing, we discard and replace. While disposability makes some things easier, it also carries a hefty environmental price tag. The disposability trend carries over into relationships, as speed dating, casual "commitments," and high divorce rates can land children and partners on the disposability heap. In the United States, about 45 percent of first marriages and over 60 percent of second marriages end in divorce.[27] In Canada and parts of Europe the rates are even higher. The disposability of families has severe consequences for the financial stability, personal health, and emotional well-being of partners, children, and society as a whole.[28] In recent years, the self-help movement, which often suggests these difficult problems have quick fixes, has burgeoned to become a $9 billion business.[29] Many of these self-help books, tapes, or workshops offer false hope with few sustained successes.[30] When desperate people seek easy solutions without doing the hard work of fundamental learning and change, resilience is undermined and real growth and learning fade.

7. **Greater hostility and enmity.** Road rage is up as people race to complete their journey ahead of others. Reality

TV shows stage win-lose battles over everything from cooking to apprenticeships, while others make us voyeurs in domestic arguments. Political dialogue is less about solving problems and more about staking out a position and being louder than one's opponent. Bipartisanship is as outdated as rotary phones and landlines. In 1976, 26.8 percent of voters in the United States lived in a county where one presidential candidate won by more than 20 percentage points. The number of people living in these "landslide counties" increased to 38 percent in 1992, to 45.3 percent in 2000, and to 48.3 percent in 2004 and 2008.[31] This partisanship indicates pockets of increasing homogeneity in our neighborhoods, reducing the opportunity to learn to get along with those who see the world differently. In personal relationships, getting our way gets in our way, as compromise and civility are replaced with contention and hostility. In work settings, we mistakenly see competing with each other as the pathway to competitive advantage. Win-lose battles crowd out win-win solutions. A false hope of the me-first mind-set is that winning will bring personal satisfaction, when it more often leads to emotional isolation. Civility and happiness come when people find delight in their work setting.

These daunting trends suggest that many people you lead face personal and societal demands that affect their well-being, their families, their communities, and inevitably their work experience. Even in the world's wealthiest nations, deficit thinking predominates. Workers at all levels respond by giving up on traditional dreams, isolating themselves, reducing their expectations, becoming dependent on government or others for support, or finding temporary escape in addictive behaviors. These responses are expensive and time consuming for employers and society. They can instigate vicious cycles of despair, withdrawal, and breakdowns in personal meaning and purpose.

And there is something organizational leaders—not just politicians, psychologists, parents, or priests—can and must do about it.

Leaders Who Focus on Meaning Create an Abundant Response

A crisis is a terrible thing to waste. Fortunately, when crises stop us in our tracks they may also make us stop and think, and thinking can be the start of creating meaning at work and elsewhere. Crises can shock us into facing the questions we often sidestep: "Who am I? What am I trying to accomplish? What really makes me happy? What do I believe? What is my purpose? What matters most?" As leaders probe the whys of work, they empower employees to find personal meaning that creates value for customers, investors, and communities.

Abundance implies plenty: enough and to spare, fullness that overflows. If we focus attention on what we stand to gain from our crises, not just what we stand to lose, abundance thinking can replace deficit thinking even when deficits are the rule of the day. Abundance looks to future opportunity more than past disappointments, promotes hope over despair, suggests change for the future rather than languishing in the past, and fosters the creation of new meaning where old meanings have broken down. Abundance does not imply that things come easily or quickly but that we can make meaning even in the midst of challenges we face. Like the Gross National Happiness index in Bhutan, the abundance we imagine is not just an abundance of visible assets (money, prestige, security, or position) but an abundance of an intangible sense of purpose, identity, growth, and well-being. To reiterate: an abundant organization is a work setting in which individuals coordinate their aspirations and actions to create meaning for themselves, value for stakeholders, and hope for humanity at large.

For our friend Rena, whose home was broken into, a focus on the things robbers could not steal—memories, loving bonds, personal skills and talents, deep religious faith, opportunities for empathy and growth—allowed Rena to shift gradually from fear-based deficit thinking to a way of life that focused on all that she had, not all she had lost. On life's goodness and personal meaning, not just on its precariousness.

Many leaders see employees' search for meaning as their own affair, while productivity and bottom-line results are the business of business. We also advocate that companies exist to get work done. In fact, rather than define an organization by its structure, roles, or rules, we define it by its capabilities: what that organization is good at doing (Apple has the capability to innovate, Disney entertains, Marriott has the capability to serve, and Walmart delivers low prices). To survive, organizations must not only amass capabilities but must also turn internal capabilities into value for external stakeholders. For-profit enterprises must create products or services that customers value and investors trust. Government agencies must meet citizen demands and respond to legislative mandates. Not-for-profit organizations continue only if they embody and further societal values. Capabilities link what goes on inside the company to what customers will pay for and what investors trust.

But in this book, we also argue that organizational capabilities more readily lead to lasting value when leaders promote meaning making as well as moneymaking. As leaders weave affirming stories, find heroes and causes, embody ethical and trusted values, clarify principles that lend order and rationality to decisions and routines, and make visible the ways employees' efforts help the company contribute to a greater good, they create organizations that overflow with a sense of meaning and abundance. In the words of former U.S. president Woodrow Wilson, "You are not here merely to make a living. You are here in order to enable the world to live more amply, with greater vision, with a finer spirit of hope and achievement. You are here to enrich the world, and you impoverish yourself if you forget the errand."[32]

Pockets of abundance can flourish in virtually any organization. The entire organization does not have to wait for a charismatic executive to push the abundance agenda. While we look to leaders to create organizational abundance, all employees also own the opportunity and responsibility to create an abundant work space for themselves and their team. Leadership is not confined to the executive suite.

As organizations become repositories of abundance, employees gain antidotes to some of the malaise, isolation, and crises of meaning discussed here. They also increase the organization's capability for doing what it does best. Apple researchers who experience abundance turn their personal creativity into Apple's product innovation. Disney "hosts" who experience abundance find a greater good in delighting theme park guests. Marriott hoteliers who experience abundance serve customers from resilient inner conviction more than easily derailed outward expedience. Walmart clerks who experience abundance can take pride in Walmart's commitment to low prices that help struggling families. While abundant organizations won't necessarily turn around divorce rates or stop drug addiction, they can be a societal force for meaning and purpose that counteracts ennui and despair both inside and outside company walls.

Whether you are an individual employee looking for a reason to get up for work every day, a manager of a team or division wanting to build employee productivity and engagement within your unit, or the leader of an entire organization committed to values, objectives, policies, results, and stories that make for great places to work, abundance is a relevant agenda. The next chapter provides an overview of seven questions and seven fields of inquiry that help promote this meaning-making, value-creating, hope-building process at all levels of organizational life.

CHAPTER 2

The Making of Abundance

bundance is neither a random act nor an isolated event. Leaders who intentionally create abundance at work build organizations that turn customer and investor expectations into daily employee actions.

Wrestling with Paradox

In Chapter 1, we introduced Vicki, whose early career enthusiasm is moderated by cutbacks and office politics; Raj, whose personal and family demands goals may temper his ability to grow his business to the next level; Grant and Shirlyn, for whom peaceful progression toward the twilight of their careers has been derailed by the current economic context; and Ivan, whose success has isolated him from himself and others. The individuals in each of these cases might say, "I've got abundance at work, all right. An abundance of headaches and hassles."

Creating abundant organizations despite headaches and hassles requires leaders to struggle with paradoxical goals and values. These individuals must balance their professional dreams, career enthusiasm, family relationships, and retirement plans against business realities, office politics, the demands of growth, and larger economic contexts. Let's face it: leaders who attend only to personal needs (theirs or their employees') may create caring organizations that end up bankrupt. On the other hand, leaders obsessed only with making money will likely be socially and emotionally bankrupt if they fail at other things that matter: reputation, relationships, sustainable purpose, engaged employees, and the simple but invaluable experience of having fun at work.

Many insightful thinkers have attended to these issues. This chapter summarizes the remainder of the book by synthesizing and integrating diverse disciplines into our definition of how leaders create personal meaning and abundant organizations.

From Turnaround to Transformation

Meeting both organizational and individual goals is seldom easy. Leaders effectively connect the two when they create a clear line of sight from employee meaning to customer and investor confidence. McKell, the CEO of a large global bank, survived the economic demands of turnaround by streamlining staff, cutting costs, managing risk, divesting toxic assets, and stabilizing profitability. McKell then realized that to go forward he needed not only to complete the economic turnaround but to begin a more fundamental transformation as well—to change how both employees and customers perceived and felt about the volatile but sometimes faceless bank.

McKell and his executive team continued to efficiently manage the bank's daily operations, but they also talked about where the bank was headed. McKell was a master of financial focus and discipline. But to put a friendly face on the bank he wanted to focus on feelings that shape meaning as well as facts that deliver results. This would mean not only continued efficiency but also relationships of trust with key clients and employees and better citizenship in the communities they served.

One of the executives jumped quickly on the bandwagon of good corporate citizenship with a proposal to invest in initiatives like microlending to underserved constituents. Another got enamored with building client trust and improving the bank's reputation for personal attention. Another felt passionate about efficiency and excellence in management processes. All three goals were ultimately about creating a sense of meaning as reflected in how people inside and out felt about their experience with the bank. And ultimately all three could help the bank's bottom line. After hours of debate McKell decided that only by embedding each of these goals in the other two would they shape a sustainable future identity. The individual values of these key executives needed to be coordinated and institutionalized for their goals to be realized.

As leaders they also needed to direct the emotional energy of employees, clients, and other stakeholders to these goals of citizenship, trust, and efficiency. Employees would need to gain a vision of how efficiency, client trust, and corporate citizenship could make their everyday jobs feel more like a personal mission and less like a duty to be endured. Clients and other stakeholders would also need a clear vision of what the bank was about and why.

When the executive team first became involved in the turnaround, they had a clear intellectual agenda for overcoming what was wrong with the bank's operations. As they began to look at transformation, however, their agenda shifted to building what was right—abundance thinking and an emergent emotional agenda. In many ways, transformation is more difficult than turnaround. In a turnaround, a pending financial crisis demands attention and thus dictates behavior. In a transformation, greater emphasis must be put on creating meaning to capture imagination and shape future behavior.

Statistics on the national economy or the corporate cash flow focus our attention on the deficits that dominate our lives, including deficits in time and money resources. But other deficits can be even more crucial to our sense of well-being—deficits in purpose, satisfying connections to other people, challenging work, resilience, and delight. Such deficits can add up to a deficit of meaning. Overcoming these deficits builds the agenda of abundance.

Discovering Meaning

Abundance is not found in circumstances or events—in how big a raise we got or how many people report to us. Abundance is found in the value we place on those events and the way we interpret their impact on us. Meaning is not inherent in events; it is made by people. This is the good news and the not-so-good news. Good news: the meaning of our lives is not controlled by what happens—as Frankl discovered, we can find purpose, value, and also happiness in a wide variety of even unpleasant circumstances. Not-so-good news: we have to work at this meaning-making process. It takes work to determine what work means, at either a corporate or a personal level. Leaders have the primary responsibility for this meaning-making process.

At a personal level, inner dialogues shape and construct this meaning. If I tell myself I'm not paid well because I'm not respected for my skills, I build a different meaning than if I tell myself how glad I am to work for an organization that is fiscally responsible. If I tell myself my boss's criticism means he is trying to help me improve because he values my contribution and wants me to succeed, I build different meaning than if I tell myself his criticism is a forerunner to my getting fired for incompetence. If I see my company as a major contributor to solving the energy crisis, I have a different feeling about the value of my labor than if I am just crunching numbers for someone else's selfish agenda. As the story goes, I feel differently about the meaning of my work if I see myself as a bricklayer than if I see myself as building a cathedral to God.

At a corporate level, leaders can help shape and construct the meaning employees assign to corporate realities, focusing corporate consciousness on opportunities instead of deficits. For example, when a corporation faces an industry downturn, people generally get nervous. Employees scramble to protect their budgets, make their own job perks sacrosanct, and push someone else between them and the corporate ax (remember Vicki's story from Chapter 1). But when leaders in one technology company made clear to employees that every $50,000 in savings could save one job, people enthusiastically rallied around cost cutting. As a result, employees were engaged, cooperative, and constructive. They had a clear line of sight between how their actions could deliver company goals while saving the jobs of people they cared about.

Because finding meaning at work is itself hard work, and because meaning is very personal, we can't promise leaders easy methods for replacing deficit thinking with abundance thinking. What we can offer leaders is a series of questions, which we will explore in the next section. We hope these questions will begin to structure conversations between leaders and their multiple constituents—conversations about what our organizations are trying to accomplish, why, and what those efforts suggest about the meaning of our lives.

These meaning-exploring questions are intended to produce the following outcomes:

o Increasing clarity about identity and signature strengths
o Gaining a sense of purpose to understand better what motivates us
o Managing work complexity through teamwork
o Replacing social isolation with positive work settings
o Identifying and responding to challenges that we care about and that engage us
o Growing from change by learning and becoming resilient
o Building sources of delight and civility into our work routines

. . . and do all this within the fiscal constraints that help keep us honest about whether we are adding real value for customers, shareholders, and communities.

Why *These* Outcomes?

The questions that produce these outcomes have emerged from our reflection on two sets of ideas. First are the societal and business challenges or crises of meaning already laid out in Chapter 1:

o Declining mental health and happiness
o Increased environmental demands that shape social responsibility, organization purpose, and individual motivation
o Increased complexity of work
o Increased isolation
o Low employee commitment
o Growing disposability
o Greater hostility and enmity

Second, a number of key concepts and even entire disciplines have arisen in response to—or at least of relevance to—these challenges. (See Figure 2.1.) The concepts we think are especially relevant to the preceding challenges are in the second column:

CHALLENGE	KEY CONCEPT AND DISCIPLINE
Mental illness and unhappiness	Positive psychology
Environmental demands	Social responsibility, organization purpose, and individual motivation
Increased complexity of work	High-performing teams
Increased isolation	Positive work environment, organization culture
Low employee commitment	Employee engagement
Disposability and change	Growth, learning, and resilience
Hostility and enmity	Civility and happiness

FIGURE 2.1 Overview of Fields and Disciplines Contributing to the Concept of Abundance

Our intent with the concept of abundant organizations is to both *synthesize* and *complement* insights and research around these key concepts, adding ideas that take each approach another step and focus it on leaders within an organizational setting. The questions and ideas that follow emerge from this synthesis. (See Table 2.1.) We provide an overview of these questions here, and the remaining chapters will probe these questions in greater detail. (See endnotes for more on the theories that provide answers to each question.)

TABLE 2.1 Abundance Summary

CHALLENGES (Crises evident in today's world)	RESPONSES (Key concepts and disciplines responding to the crises)	PRINCIPLES OF ABUNDANCE (Synthesis and **extension of current thinking**)
DECLINING MENTAL HEALTH AND HAPPINESS Increasing rates of depression, anxiety, and addiction, resulting in higher cost of benefits and lost productivity	**POSITIVE PSYCHOLOGY** Focus on what is right, not what is wrong; identify and build on signature strengths	Build on strengths (capabilities in an organization) **that strengthen others**
INCREASED ENVIRONMENTAL DEMANDS (SOCIAL, TECH-NOLOGICAL, ECONOMIC, POLITICAL, ENVIRONMEN-TAL, DEMOGRAPHIC) A shrinking pool of natural resources and an erosion of trust in large institutions	**SOCIAL RESPONSIBILITY/ ORGANIZATION PURPOSE/ INDIVIDUAL MOTIVATION** Include social responsibility as part of organization purpose and individual motivation	Have organization purposes that sustain both social and **fiscal responsibility and align organization purposes and individual motivation**
INCREASED COMPLEXITY OF WORK Technology, globalization, and demographics create more complex work environments	**HIGH-PERFORMING TEAMS** Understand dimensions of a high-performing team	Make high-performing teams **high-relating teams**
INCREASED ISOLATION Increasing numbers of people who live in social isolation from each other; the erosion of neighborhoods and social groups	**POSITIVE WORK ENVIRONMENTS** Create positive work cultures through stories, rituals, and policies	Create positive work cultures **that affirm and connect people throughout the organization**
LOW EMPLOYEE COMMITMENT A large percentage of employees feel disconnected from their firm, resulting in lower customer satisfaction and productivity	**EMPLOYEE ENGAGEMENT** Create work processes that engage employees	Develop employees' competence and engage their commitment, **but also shape their sense of contribution**

continued

TABLE 2.1 Abundance Summary *(continued)*

CHALLENGES (Crises evident in today's world)	RESPONSES (Key concepts and disciplines responding to the crises)	PRINCIPLES OF ABUNDANCE (Synthesis and **extension of current thinking**)
DISPOSABILITY AND CHANGE Lack of long-term commitments to people and things leads to leaving, not learning	**GROWTH, LEARNING, AND RESILIENCE** Bounce back after setbacks and create a learning culture	In the face of change, use principles of growth, learning, and resilience **to persevere with both people and products**
HOSTILITY AND ENMITY Win-lose paradigms crowd out win-win solutions.	**CIVILITY** Demonstrate respect by honoring and valuing differences	Honor differences **in what helps individuals feel happy, cared for, and excited about life**

Seven Questions That Drive Abundance

We propose seven questions to help leaders drive the abundance agenda—questions that help leaders make meaning, add value, create emotional energy, and foster hope while at work. These questions apply to leaders at the personal level (Am I finding abundance myself?), at the interpersonal level (Do we have an abundant work team?), at the organization level (Are we fostering abundance in this organization?), and at the societal level (Can our industry or community help humanity at large?). The key concepts listed on the right in the preceding list help us approach these questions. The key principles of an abundant organization emerge from these approaches. This is the architecture for abundance.

1. What Am I Known For? (Identity)

A sense of abundance is fostered by a clear sense of who we are, what we believe in, and what we are good at. In the bank example, McKell and his team were excited when they shaped their organization's future identity around efficiency, trust, and citizenship. They then had to turn this corporate identity or brand into personal action among the 30,000-plus bank employees.

Chapter 3 describes how leaders can shape an organization-wide identity and then help individuals use their personal strengths to foster that identity and succeed at work. It also describes how leaders shape organizational strengths (capabilities) to build an abundant corporate identity or brand, turning external stakeholder expectations into internal corporate actions.

The field of positive psychology helps leaders answer this primary question. The traditional approach of psychology to depression, anxiety, and addiction disorders has been to develop models and techniques for fixing what is wrong with us. Few theorists or clinicians also probed what is right. Into this space, Martin Seligman and his associates have inserted the proposal that the domain of psychology extends beyond fixing pathology to probing health and happiness.[1] Positive psychology asks what makes people happy in the long run. Researchers in positive psychology have discovered that when we identify and regularly use our signature character strengths, life becomes more satisfying and meaningful.[2] They further assert that even when we must cope with depression, anxiety, addiction, or other mental illness (and their corporate equivalents), building on our signature strengths fosters creativity and courage for tackling our challenges.

The abundant organization adapts principles of positive psychology to help leaders build both organizational strengths and the strengths of individual employees.[3] In addition, we propose that leaders in abundant organizations not only recognize and build on strengths but also use those strengths to create value for external stakeholders. At both personal and organizational levels, the meaning we find from our strengths deepens as we not only build on our strengths but build on strengths that strengthen others too.

PRINCIPLE (1)

Abundant organizations build on strengths (capabilities in an organization) that strengthen others.

2. Where Am I Going? (Purpose and Motivation)

Abundance emerges from a clear sense of what we are trying to accomplish and why. Too often employees' and employers' goals are at cross-purposes, resulting in both individual frustration and organizational underperformance due to employee cynicism and lack of perceived corporate vision. As McKell and his team worked through the paradoxical goals of trust, efficiency, and citizenship, they created a sense of corporate purpose that helped employees fulfill their personal purposes through their work at the bank. Employees who can meet their personal goals at work remain motivated and engaged; those who can't, go in a different direction, physically or emotionally.

Chapter 4 offers suggestions for how leaders create purposeful organizations that help employees' personal ambitions match organizational goals. When our personal goals align with the organization's goals, work feels like a meaningful extension of our private journey. As we both own and personalize our company's mission, we find opportunities to impact broad societal problems we care about.

Social responsibility and environmental activism are fields that speak to the importance of addressing society's biggest problems while investing in corporate citizenship. To manage scarce resources and rebuild organization reputations, many leaders have begun to pay attention to a "triple bottom line" of people (values and reputation), profits (financial return), and planet (e.g., carbon footprint).[4] Environmental activists help corporations audit their carbon footprints and reduce energy consumption. Other organizations demonstrate a caring heart as they invest in philanthropic initiatives. These citizenship efforts underscore values of stewardship and accountability that help employees see how their personal values align with corporate values to make a real difference in the real world.

Just as the bank had to balance profit, purpose, and people, leaders in the abundant organization focus on sustainable profit as well as environmental sustainability. An organization that emphasizes social contribution without facing the economic realities of creating value for customers and investors will not survive. While bankruptcy will certainly reduce an organization's carbon footprint, it will also eliminate its ability to employ workers, make useful products, offer customers innovative solutions, and build communities.

PRINCIPLE 2

Abundant organizations have purposes that sustain both social and fiscal responsibility and align individual motivation.

3. Whom Do I Travel With? (Relationships and Teamwork [Th]at Work)

Our sense of abundance is enhanced by meaningful relationships. The increasing complexities of today's workplaces require combining people with different skills into cohesive and high-performing teams. As McKell and his team worked to shape the bank's direction, they found that their ability to work as a team turned individual strengths into organization capabilities. When they put aside individual biases for the good of the overall bank, they made the whole of the team more than the sum of the individual players. They worked to create this sense of teamwork throughout the organization.

Chapter 5 suggests specific ways leaders can strengthen positive work relationships that enhance teamwork. These work relationships make even difficult work more doable. Our meaningful work relationships include friendships, mentoring relationships, and professional networks.[5] Research on high-performing teams explores the ways teams coordinate the efforts of many people to solve complex problems. Although teamwork is itself more complicated than working alone, it also allows team members to reduce complexity by specializing. Research suggests that high-performing teams operate with clear purposes, good governance, positive team member relationships, and the ability to learn.[6]

While leaders must attend to teamwork in complex work settings, the concept of abundant organizations goes beyond teams that produce and perform their tasks well to teams that engender a kind of passion that allows for creativity, focused energy, trusting connections, and mutual respect. High-performing teams come from high-relating people. Research on successful marriages suggests patterns and stages of effective long-term committed relationships that can be applied to teams in organization settings. The best teams work through these stages and use these patterns to combat "organization divorce" characterized by burnout, turnover, and lost productivity. When leaders help their organization "families" move beyond the superficialities of getting along to struggling through conflict so that they can understand one another's strengths and weaknesses, they can approach the kind of synergy that occurs in the best of human relationships. They gain a competitive advantage over a less relationally sophisticated competitor. This means that leaders need to learn and model the skills of building good relationships at work. Lynda Gratton has captured this sense of team cohesiveness with the term *glow*, which includes a cooperative mind-set, jumping across boundaries, and igniting latent energy.[7]

PRINCIPLE 3

Abundant organizations take work relationships beyond high-performing teams to high-relating teams.

4. How Do I Build a Positive Work Environment? (Effective Work Culture or Setting)

Abundance thrives on positive routines that help ground us in what matters most. While bad habits thrive on isolation and shame, positive routines help us connect with ourselves and others. As McKell and his team focused on their future identity, they wanted to establish a culture focused on building what is right, not just eliminating what is wrong. They wanted to replace backbiting with forward thinking, politics with collaboration, and self-interest with other-directed service.

Chapter 6 suggests ways leaders can create and sustain positive routines to foster effectiveness, efficiency, and meaningful connection. Leaders can tolerate cynical, negative, and demeaning cultures, or they can encourage constructive, affirming, and uplifting cultures. Leaders shape these cultures through their words and deeds. These cultures replace individual isolation with corporate connection.

Leaders who engender positive work environments promote good communication, development opportunities, and pleasant physical facilities to ensure a positive culture at work. Instead of building routines and patterns that encourage self-reflection, honest sharing, and the kind of consistency that brings people together, many of us build habits, addictions, and compulsive patterns that serve primarily to block out other people. Or we build almost no routines at all, leaving us untethered in time and space and making us unpredictable to those who want to connect. Routines and patterns driven by our deepest values help us stay grounded in what matters most and available to those who matter most. When leaders support individual and policy-level routines that help work *work*, they create a positive environment that both sustains productivity and fosters connection.[8]

Workplaces of all kinds use checklists and routines to ensure quality control. Checklists and routines that are chosen personally around core values and relationships lend predictability and stability to our lives. Instead of constantly fighting against time and space, we work with them in a mindful, realistic way. Whether personally or organizationally, flexible but consistent routines can help us know ourselves and others while countering both the perfectionism and the unpredictability that get in the way of connection.

PRINCIPLE (4)

Abundant organizations create positive work environments that affirm and connect people throughout the organization.

5. What Challenges Interest Me? (Personalized Contributions)

It is hard to imagine abundance in the absence of challenge. The most engaged employees are generally those whose work gives them the opportunity to stretch while doing work they love and solving problems they care about. The bank executives gave employees a new challenge when they shifted the focus from turnaround to transformation through efficiency, trust, and citizenship. These three pillars of the bank's identity challenged employees to solve problems they cared about.

As leaders involve both teams and individuals in enjoyable challenges, they engage employees' hearts and their minds, as Chapter 7 discusses. Different people find different kinds of work easy, energizing, and enjoyable and different problems meaningful. Leaders need to adapt broad general challenges to individual requirements and predispositions.

The study of talent has evolved from a focus on employee competence (*ability* to do the work) to employee commitment (*willingness* to do the work).[9] Employees who are competent but not committed will not perform to their full potential. Commitment comes from building an employee value proposition that engages employees to use their discretionary energy to pursue organization goals.[10] Commitment or engagement grows when we work in a company with a vision, have opportunities to learn and grow, do work that has an impact, receive fair pay for work done, work with people we like working with, and enjoy flexibility in the terms and conditions of work.

43

Leaders in abundant organizations take employee competence and commitment another step—to employee contribution. Contribution focuses not just on activity but on the meaningfulness of the activity. For example, a teenager may be highly competent at video games (he wins them often), have a high commitment to video games (shown by playing them for hours at a time), but still not find real purpose and meaning in game playing. An employee may be competent (able to do the work) and committed (willing to work hard), but not have the sense of abundance that comes from also making a contribution to a greater good.

PRINCIPLE (5)

Abundance occurs when companies can engage not only employees' skills (competence) and loyalty (commitment) but also their values (contribution).

6. How Do I Respond to Disposability and Change? (Growth, Learning, and Resilience)

Abundance acknowledges that failure can be a powerful impetus to growth and learning. When we face change and take risks to work outside our comfort zone, resist defensiveness about mistakes, learn from failure, and keep trying, we become not only more resilient but also more satisfied with life. McKell and his team knew that as they tried to implement their new organization identity and purpose they would make mistakes. Instead of hiding from and finding someone to blame for mistakes, they committed to facing and learning from them.

Chapter 8 reviews how leaders can encourage learning and resilience. Abundance is less about getting things right and more about moving in the right direction. Resilience reflects a positive outlook on work and shapes learning for the future rather than lamenting the past.[11]

Research on personal resilience and learning organizations offers exciting insights into what helps people and institutions endure in the face of both suffering and setbacks. By studying what helps POWs survive and thrive, how Navy Seals can be trained to stay calm under attack, and what abused children who become successful have in common, we get hints about how leaders encourage learning under conditions of stress and challenge.

Unlike the assumption of disposability that governs so much of modern society, resilience and learning principles challenge us to "repair, reuse, and recycle" people, products, and programs rather than tossing them. In tough economic environments organizations will necessarily reduce staff, drop products, and cut nonessential programs; nevertheless, hiring freezes and reduced funds for research and development also mean we must work with whom and what we have. Abundance means we not only learn attitudes of resilience that help us thrive under stress; we also use these principles to make do with what we have. As we do so we come to realize that what we have is actually enough.

PRINCIPLE (6)

Abundant organizations use principles of growth, learning, and resilience to respond to change.

7. What Delights Me? (Civility and Happiness)

Abundance thrives on simple pleasures. Sources of delight might include laughing at ourselves, appreciating excellence, relishing beauty, being present in the moment, and having fun at work.[12] As McKell and his team laid out the bank's new identity, they encouraged employees to have fun in shaping this identity. Corporate fun included contests, celebrations, and communications about the new direction.

When leaders encourage civility and delight in how work is done, they go a long way toward creating a sense of abundance, as shown in Chapter 9. These sources of delight are highly personal, depending on the personality of the leader and the requirements of the employees.

The hostility rampant in modern life is itself under fire these days. The cry for tolerance demands that we outgrow our racial, religious, political, ethnic, and gender stereotypes. The cry for civility also calls on us to outgrow our we-they, win-lose, right-wrong, blame-and-shame mentality. As we move away from hostility and blame toward problem solving, listening, curiosity, and compassion, simple civility greases the skids.

Under the rubric of valuing differences, leaders are encouraged to understand, respect, and learn from the perspectives of people of different races, genders, backgrounds, or even professional training, replacing hostility with civility. We may also want to look for and rejoice in the different ways people find sweetness in life, going beyond civility to delight. Sensitivity to such differences helps us find a wide variety of ways to bring pleasure and delight into the workplace. For some perhaps a celebration of 10 years of service is meaningful; for others a renewing sense of delight is evoked by a note from the boss, a compliment, a shared joke, a favorite song, a different chair, a new dish at lunch, or simply a beautiful sunset shared on the way to the parking lot. Delight often comes in small packages, and when money is tight it helps to know that small and simple pleasures spread over time have more impact on our sense of well-being than grand one-time gestures.[13]

PRINCIPLE (7)

Abundant organizations attend not only to outward demographic diversity but also to the diversity of what makes individuals feel happy, cared for, and excited about life.

Organizational Application

Much of what brings meaning into our personal and professional lives can be categorized under the preceding seven headings. When leaders help employees explore these questions, they help create abundant organizations with positive individual and organization results:

○ Higher commitment, better employee health, improved productivity and retention[14]
○ A leadership brand that builds investor confidence[15]
○ Increased customer commitment (because customer attitudes about an organization correlate with the attitudes of its employees)
○ Increased investor confidence in future earnings and higher market value (based on intangible assets like leadership and quality of employees)
○ Improved community reputation, merited by stronger social responsibility.

Table 2.2 provides an organizational assessment tool for abundance to help leaders parse out the components of

TABLE 2.2 Assessment of the Abundant Organization

Think of the organization where you work as you complete the following assessment. In a small company, this would be the entire organization; in a large company, it would be a division, plant, geography, or other work unit.

PRINCIPLES OF ABUNDANT ORGANIZATIONS	ABUNDANT ORGANIZATION QUESTIONS *To what extent does my organization . . .*	ASSESSMENT *1 = lo; 5 = hi*
IDENTITY: WHAT ARE WE KNOWN FOR? Build on strengths (capabilities in an organization) that strengthen others	1. Have a clear identity around what we are known for that is shared by those inside and outside the organization?	
	2. Focus on key individual strengths (or organization capabilities) that distinguish us in our markets?	
	3. Encourage employees to use their signature strengths at work to strengthen others?	
PURPOSE AND DIRECTION: WHERE ARE WE GOING? Have purposes that sustain both social and fiscal responsibility	4. Communicate its social purpose and organizational direction with clarity and consistency?	
	5. Match employees' personal goals with the organization purpose?	
	6. Help employees achieve what motivates them?	
TEAMWORK/RELATIONSHIPS: HOW WELL DO WE TRAVEL TOGETHER? Go beyond high-performing teams to high-relating teams	7. Bring team members together to solve problems and make decisions?	
	8. Foster teamwork that delivers creative outcomes?	
	9. Enable people to form positive relationships and resolve conflict?	

PRINCIPLES OF ABUNDANT ORGANIZATIONS	ABUNDANT ORGANIZATION QUESTIONS *To what extent does my organization . . .*	ASSESSMENT *1 = lo; 5 = hi*
ENGAGEMENT/CHALLENGING WORK: WHAT CHALLENGES INTEREST EMPLOYEES? Engage not only employees' heads (competence) and hands (commitment) but also their hearts (contribution)	10. Encourage employees to choose work projects that challenge them?	
	11. Allow flexibility in how work is done ?	
	12. Help employees see how their work positively impacts others?	
EFFECTIVE CONNECTIONS: HOW DO WE DEMONSTRATE A POSITIVE WORK ENVIRONMENT? Create work cultures that affirm and connect people throughout the organization	13. Demonstrate a positive rather than a cynical work environment?	
	14. Use time and space to build patterns of affirmation and connection?	
	15. Provide resources to help every person meet the demands of his or her job?	
RESILIENCE: HOW DO WE LEARN AND GROW FROM CHANGE? Respond to change by mastering principles of growth, learning, and resilience	16. Persevere to develop people and products?	
	17. Encourage learning from both successes and setbacks?	
	18. Recover when things go wrong?	
CIVILITY AND DELIGHT: HOW DO WE BRING DELIGHT INTO OUR ORGANIZATION? Attend to what helps individuals feel happy, cared for, and excited about life	19. Feel like a friendly place?	
	20. Encourage employees to have fun at work?	
	21. Demonstrate respect and civility for all?	

If you score 85–105, you are in an abundant work setting. Relish it; work to make it last.

If you score 70–84, your work setting is on track to make abundance happen. Identify the questions where you score lower and focus on them.

If you score 55–69, you are close to losing it.

If you score less than 54, your organization's journey to abundance may be nigh impossible at the present time. If you are committed to staying at your organization, find one or two areas where you can make progress. Don't try to do it all at once.

For more information on these surveys and other assessments, go to thewhyofwork.com.

abundant organizations and assess areas of strength and weakness. The remaining chapters of this book will address each area in more detail. These chapters will give leaders specific tools and concepts for increasing organizational abundance in teams, divisions, or companies.

These principles apply at a personal level as well, as shown in Table 2.3. Questions on this individual assessment tool can help you and individuals you work with gauge your sense of *personal* abundance and meaning at work. You will find more specific tools and concepts for increasing your personal sense of abundance at work in the chapters that follow.

Getting high scores on these questions does not mean that work will suddenly feel easy, people will get along instantly, customers will flock to buy products, or stock prices will soar overnight. Meaning does not ensure ease; it offers hope. Playwright and founding president of the Czech Republic, Václav Havel, writes, "Hope is not prognostication . . . It is not the conviction that something will turn out well, but the certainty that something makes sense, regardless of how it turns out." Abundance emerges from the growing conviction that what we are about "makes sense"—that it contributes to something larger than ourselves and that it is grounded in our deepest values. Such conviction does not forestall all problems, but it helps us confront problems with courage and integrity. And it is in that confrontation that meaning—abundance—flourishes.

In economically good times, abundant organizations matter. In tough times, they matter even more. When organizations address the key questions and build on the guiding principles of abundance, capable, committed employees also have the satisfaction of knowing their work makes a genuine contribution. Customers receive products and services that meet their needs. Investors have more confidence in the company's future. Communities and ecologies are sustained responsibly.

In short, there is enough. And to spare.

TABLE 2.3 Assessment of Individual Abundance at Work

Think about your current personal experience with work as you complete the following assessment.

PRINCIPLES OF ABUNDANT ORGANIZATIONS	PERSONAL ABUNDANCE QUESTIONS *To what extent do I . . .*	ASSESSMENT *1 = lo; 5 = hi*
IDENTITY: WHAT AM I KNOWN FOR? Build on strengths (capabilities in an organization) that strengthen others	1. Have a clear identity at work with which I feel comfortable?	
	2. Spend more energy at work contributing from my strengths than tackling my weaknesses?	
	3. Use my signature strengths (core character traits) at work to strengthen others?	
PURPOSE AND DIRECTION: WHERE AM I GOING? Make sure organization purpose links social responsibility and individual motivation	4. Feel invested in the social purposes and direction of my organization?	
	5. Feel my personal goals are in line with the organization's purposes?	
	6. Do my part to build profitability and use corporate resources wisely?	
TEAMWORK: WHOM DO I TRAVEL WITH? Go beyond high-performing teams to high-relating teams	7. Help my work team stay focused on solving problems and making decisions?	
	8. Foster teamwork that delivers creative outcomes?	
	9. Pay attention to the social and emotional needs of my team members?	

continued

TABLE 2.3 Assessment of Individual Abundance at Work *(continued)*

PRINCIPLES OF ABUNDANT ORGANIZATIONS	PERSONAL ABUNDANCE QUESTIONS *To what extent do I . . .*	ASSESSMENT *1 = lo; 5 = hi*
ENGAGEMENT/ CHALLENGING WORK: WHAT CHALLENGES INTEREST ME? Engage not only employees' heads (competence) and hands (commitment), but also their hearts (contribution)	10. Find ways to organize my work around challenges that I enjoy?	
	11. Maintain the skills and commitment to be effective at work?	
	12. Conceptualize my work around impacting others in ways that are meaningful to me?	
EFFECTIVE CONNECTIONS: HOW DO I BUILD A POSITIVE WORK ENVIRONMENT? Create work cultures that affirm and connect people throughout the organization	13. Contribute to a positive rather than a cynical work environment?	
	14. Use my time and space to build patterns of affirmation and connection with others?	
	15. Negotiate for the physical, emotional, and social resources I need to meet the demands of my job?	
RESILIENCE: HOW DO I LEARN FROM CHANGE? Persevere by mastering principles of growth, learning, and resilience	16. Persevere to develop people I work with and products I work on?	
	17. Learn nondefensively from both successes and setbacks?	
	18. Recover when things go wrong?	
CIVILITY AND DELIGHT: WHAT DELIGHTS ME? Attend to what helps individuals feel happy, cared for, and excited about life	19. Promote friendly interactions at work?	
	20. Have fun at work?	
	21. Demonstrate respect and civility for all people I work with?	

If you score 85–105, you have an abundant work life. Relish it; work to make it last.

If you score 70–84, you are on track to make your work abundant. Identify the questions where you score lower and focus on them.

If you score 55–69, you are close to losing it.

If you score less than 54, your work efforts may not be leading you to abundance. If you are committed to staying at your organization, find one or two areas where you can make progress. Don't try to do it all at once.

For more information on these surveys and other assessments, go to thewhyofwork.com.

CHAPTER 3

What Am I Known For? (Identity)

LEADERSHIP **IDENTITY** CHALLENGE

With rapid technological, demographic, political, and social change, organizations scramble to align employee strengths into a coherent organization identity that responds to evolving customer and societal requirements. Great leaders help individuals align their personal strengths with the organization identity (firm brand) and with customer expectations.

J ason Bourne is on the run (hear the insistent beat of the background music). Although struggling to clear a fog of amnesia about his history, he has not forgotten how to fight bad guys, break into Swiss banks, blow up cars, perform emergency medical procedures, gain the trust of wary women, or speak Russian, although he has no idea where he learned these things or why he needed to know them. Haunted by violent images, aware that others are out to get him, and spooked by his own instinctive capacities, he is horrified by the conclusion pressing upon him: he must be a killer for hire. Bourne has all the skills of a cold and highly trained assassin, but his moral values are deeply offended by such a possibility.

Jason Bourne is a fictional character: a highly skilled operative for an imaginary secret government agency gone bad, an agency that recruited him for his talent and patriotism, an agency he turns against and turns in as he realizes its corrupt leadership has deceived him. His predicament provides an interesting reminder that our identity does not consist only of the name we use, the stories we remember, or the people we know. Our identity is grounded in how we instinctively use our skills in the service of our deepest values. Although our lives do not play out to driving rhythms in tightly edited chase scenes, each of us is trying to figure out who we are, to analyze what we do well and whether it serves our deepest values.

At both a personal and an organizational level, a meaningful life is one that expresses who we are as articulately and honestly as possible, both with our words and through our actions. Who we are is not just about what we can do; it is about what we love and what we hate, what we desire and what we fear, what we know and what we are still trying to figure out. It is not enough for Jason Bourne to be good at what he does, even in the service of his own survival. He needs to know what end his skills serve, and he yearns for that end to be something he deeply believes in. When his institutional identity clashes with his personal identity, even when he cannot remember exactly why, his loyalty is lost and the institution he once served becomes the enemy.

Great leaders understand that the search for meaning that builds abundance is grounded in clarity about our truest individual and organizational values and how they align. Such leaders claim their values through their life choices and help others do the same. This is the beginning of an authentic and meaningful organizational experience.

Signature Strengths and Capabilities

When we meet people, we often categorize them by where they work, what they wear, how they smile, or how they speak. These are at best superficial indicators of real values and competencies. Underneath our role, profession, appearance, or observable talents are what psychologists call *signature strengths*: the character traits and values most central to who we are. Psychologists hypothesize that some core virtues are valued by virtually every culture and philosophy. (Examples would be gratitude, humility, courage, compassion, fairness, integrity, humor, forgiveness, and love of learning.) While we may agree that all such traits are important, typically we especially espouse and want to be known for a few. These signature strengths are likely to persist regardless of our role, profession, appearance, or talents. We also have skills, talents, and knowledge that are so embedded as to be instinctive, but our signature strengths are not just about talents and skills. Signature strengths are grounded in the moral values we espouse, the virtues we cherish. Like Bourne, we feel at odds with ourselves when our skills, however proficient, are not used in the service of our signature strengths—our deepest personal values.

Organizations also have identities and project images that shape the perceptions of both customers and employees. We call an organization's signature strengths its capabilities—what that organization does best in the service of its core purposes. Perhaps part of the success of *The Bourne Identity* as a novel and a movie was its ability to capture the crisis we all face when our personal identity is at odds with that of an organization we once trusted and devoted ourselves to.

On a lighter note, Dave once did some consulting for Harley-Davidson, and the company kindly gave him a Harley-Davidson signature leather jacket. The jacket embodied all it meant to be Harley-Davidson: tough, fast, wild, and hard around the edges. Dave had fun wearing the jacket because it changed how others perceived him. No more Mister Nice Guy! Then our quiet, academically oriented 16-year-old daughter found the jacket. She wore it to school one day. She came home and said, "I met guys today I never knew existed before." We hid the jacket!

Harley owners have an identity that shows up in their clothes and actions. They are proud of their affiliation with the Harley brand, which aligns with their desired identity and values. Companies can spend millions of dollars creating and communicating these brand identities through creative marketing. Nike's swoosh stands for athletes in action; Walmart trucks and ads carry the slogan "always low prices"; the BP tagline bears the standard for "beyond petroleum" as BP tries to move into alternative energy sources. In the best companies, these public identities also translate into management actions inside the organization. Nike's corporate headquarters boasts gyms, tracks, and weight rooms, which employees are encouraged to use. Walmart holds executive retreats in modest surroundings to maintain its cost consciousness. BP leaders look for opportunities to work on energy outside traditional petroleum sources. Good companies know their signature strengths and their capabilities and align their services and their management practices with them. A company brand presents a point of view about the company, proposes a lifestyle consistent with that point of view, and shapes customer expectations.

Sometimes when employees' signature strengths intersect with the signature capabilities of their workplaces there is a seamless fit; other times there is a clash of values and goals. Have you ever been in an organization where you felt out of place? This happened when we entered an exclusive clothing shop on Rodeo Drive in Beverly Hills. We clearly did not belong. We knew it, and the staff knew it. Our personal identity did not mesh with their corporate identity. We would have needed more than a complete wardrobe overhaul to work in such a place; we would have needed a complete overhaul of our personal signature strengths.

As a leader, you create a more abundant organization when you help employees clarify their personal identity and enhance their signature strengths and then help them see how those strengths fit with the goals and values of the organization. As diagrammed in Figure 3.1, the steps in this process are:

1. Help employees define and grow their personal strengths.
2. Define and build organizational capabilities required for success.
3. Meld personal strengths and organizational capabilities.

FIGURE 3.1   Melding Individual, Organization, and Customer Identity

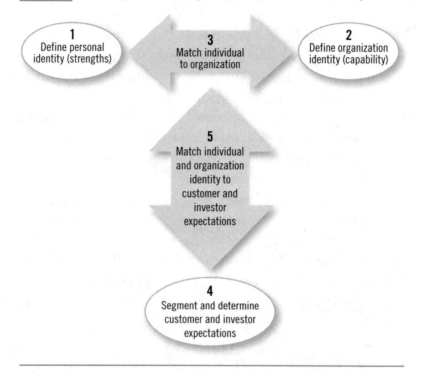

4. Determine customer and investor expectations.
5. Connect both personal and organizational identities
    with the needs of customers and investors.

We'll look at these five steps in more detail.

1. Help Employees Define and Grow
Their Personal Strengths

How does a leader help someone identify and build personal
strengths? If deficit thinking focuses us on what is missing,

abundance thinking focuses us on what is available and possible. As leaders we want to focus employees' attention on the latter, including a focus on their own identities.

Self-awareness is capricious. At times we are very aware of our flaws. When we look in the mirror, the zits or wrinkles jump out and overshadow our strong chin or fetching eyes. Not only do we magnify our flaws; we also ignore the strengths we have. Those with curly hair buy straightening irons; those with straight hair get perms. We once asked a group of young people to share what they saw as their physical flaws. One young man admitted sheepishly that his ears stuck out, which really bothered him. No one else in the group had ever noticed his ears sticking out. Even when this "flaw" was called to their attention, it quickly fell to the background when they interacted with him.

At other times we tend to flee from our flaws. Leadership researchers find that most leaders are better at identifying their strengths than their weaknesses. We run and hide from things we do not do well, out of embarrassment or uncertainty about how to change. Realism about both our strengths and our weaknesses is essential to a strengths-based identity. Great leaders build on their strengths but also bring their weaknesses to at least neutral. They help employees and companies to do the same.

Realism can hurt, but it also helps us invest our energy where it has the best chance of paying off. When Dave was younger, he liked basketball and played with enthusiasm. He had a dream that one day he might play college or even pro basketball. While this dream led him to hours of dedicated practice, it also gave him false hope. He eventually realized that he did not have the raw physical talent for professional basketball. He could continue to find great fun in community pickup games and watching others play, but being a professional athlete was not his strength. When Dave realized that he had other strengths that would give meaning to his life and pursued them with the same work ethic and enthusiasm (his real and enduring "signature strengths"), he was able to find sustainable meaning in his work.

When you as a leader help employees develop honest self-perceptions, you help them invest in the real dreams that bring meaning to life. You can help employees discover their identity through formal assessments, informal observations, conversations, and assignments.

Formal Assessments

Until we name and use them, we often take our strengths for granted. Innumerable personality tests depict who we are as colors, types, styles, initials, or aptitudes. Recently, two sets of scholars have worked to synthesize categories of strengths or core values that define us.

○ **Seligman and his colleagues.** Martin Seligman, the father of positive psychology, has identified six domains of personal strengths and 24 individual character traits within those domains. (See Figure 3.2.) As you look over this list, you may have a pretty good idea of which traits you value and exhibit most. Seligman's research suggests that people get a boost in personal happiness when they use their signature strengths regularly and in new and creative ways. When we deliberately structure our work and our interactions to build on our signature strengths, we feel like we have enough and to spare of what it takes to do the job at hand. (If you want a more scientific

FIGURE 3.2 Seligman's Signature Strengths

WISDOM AND KNOWLEDGE—cognitive strengths in acquiring and using knowledge
1. Curiosity—appreciating novelty and ambiguity; inquisitive
2. Love of Learning—enjoying reading and experiences that enhance knowledge
3. Open-mindedness—looking at all sides of an issue; critical thinking skill
4. Creativity—thinking about things in new ways; ingenuity at problem solving
5. Perspective—ability to see the big picture; objectivity

COURAGE—emotional strengths of accomplishing goals in the face of opposition
6. Bravery—facing physical or social danger despite fear; taking difficult stands
7. Perseverance—finishing what one starts without getting sidetracked
8. Authenticity—keeping one's word; being honest, genuine, and authentic
9. Zeal—throwing oneself into life; having zest and passion about one's activities

TEMPERANCE—emotional strengths that protect against excesses
10. Self-regulation—controlling one's emotions and behaviors; self-disciplined
11. Prudence—exercising caution, resisting impulses that impede long-term goals
12. Forgiveness—giving others a second chance; letting go of revenge
13. Modesty—unpretentiousness; downplaying one's own importance

HUMANITY—interpersonal strengths that provide closeness and care for others
14. Kindness and generosity—caring for others; empathy; volunteering; a desire to help
15. Social intelligence—fitting in with others; awareness of others' feelings
16. Loving and accepting love—valuing closeness; ability to both give and receive love

JUSTICE—interpersonal strengths that support healthy communities
17. Teamwork—loyalty; citizenship; a sense of duty and commitment to the group
18. Fairness—treating others equally even if they are different or disadvantaged
19. Leadership—organizing and motivating others while maintaining good relationships

continued

FIGURE 3.2 Seligman's Signature Strengths *(continued)*

TRANSCENDENCE—spiritual strengths that connect us to the universe and provide meaning

20. Appreciation of beauty and excellence—delight in nature, art, skill, or excellence
21. Gratitude—counting one's blessings; expressing thanks; delighting in life's goodness
22. Hope—expecting good outcomes and a positive future based on effort today
23. Humor and playfulness—ability to have fun, play, joke, and make others smile
24. Religiousness—a strong belief system; feeling connected to God

---

accounting, go to authentichappiness.org and take the *VIA Survey of Character Strengths* to identify your signature strengths compared to other people. Use of this research site is free and can be used by you and your work team to determine and compare your strengths.)

○ **Gallup organization.** Marcus Buckingham and colleagues in his firm and the Gallup organization have also developed an instrument that helps people assess work-related skills and characteristics. They find that such skills are difficult to train for but easier to hire for. They have identified 34 strengths a leader should consider when hiring an individual for a job—strengths that have little to do with specific work experience or job skill but a lot to do with the qualities it would take to work well in a specific culture or with a certain kind of customer. We list these strengths in Figure 3.3. (To take their test, buy *Now, Discover Your Strengths* to obtain a code for the online test.)

As a leader, you might invite employees to take either (or both) of these tests as a way to quantify what comes naturally to them. While self-assessments have a certain self-bias, they still offer us a strengths language that facilitates discussion and self-awareness. They help employees see patterns that inform their identity. They also help you as a leader know what types of opportunities your employees are most likely to take joy and pride in at work.

FIGURE 3.3 Buckingham's Strengthfinder Attributes

Achiever	Driving relentlessly to get things done and to accomplish
Activator	Getting started quickly to take action on decisions
Adaptability	Flexing and responding to the demands of the moment
Analytical	Looking for patterns, questioning, objective, data-driven
Arranger	Jumping in to manage all the variables and find the best layout
Belief	Maintaining strong core values around family, spirituality, altruism
Command	Taking charge and getting others on board despite risks, differences
Communication	Bringing ideas to life through writing, speaking, focusing
Competition	Measuring performance by comparing and winning
Connectedness	Seeing how everything and everyone is connected, interdependent
Context	Looking to the past, the context, for answers about today
Deliberative	Being cautious, vigilant, aware of risks, and serious about handling risks
Developer	Seeing potential in others and enjoy helping them grow
Discipline	Liking routines and structures to maintain productivity
Empathy	Tuning in to others' feelings and viewpoints
Fairness	Treating everyone equally and by consistent rules
Focus	Being goal-driven and tangent-avoidant
Futuristic	Imagining the future with hope and vision
Harmony	Looking for agreement and avoiding conflict
Ideation	Getting energized by ideas, connections, insights
Inclusiveness	Bringing others in and valuing commonality over differences
Individualization	Valuing what is unique and special about each person

continued

FIGURE **3.3**   Buckingham's Strengthfinder Attributes *(continued)*

Input	Acquiring and filing away ideas, things, relationships, images
Intellection	Liking to think, introspect, reflect in private
Learner	Loving the process of learning and always being engaged in it
Maximizer	Driving toward excellence and making something the best it can be
Positivity	Praising generously, seeing what is right, optimism
Relater	Delighting in close friends and deepening relationships
Responsibility	Conscientiously focusing on doing what you promise
Restorative	Liking to solve problems, facilitate healing, fix things
Self-assurance	Having deep confidence in your strengths, abilities, judgment
Significance	Desiring recognition, admiration as a credible professional
Strategic	Seeing the consequences and contingencies to chart a course
WOO	"Winning Others Over" through getting others to like you

Observations

To rephrase an old axiom, "We judge ourselves by our intentions, but others judge us by our behavior." While tests offer a quick way to identify how we view our strengths, other people are often more interested in our performance than in our intentions or dreams. When our son was in eighth grade, he came home excited and thrilled with his report card. We were anxious to see his grades and share his enthusiasm. He proudly displayed the report card boasting an A, B, C, D, and F. Our enthusiasm quickly waned. He explained that he had spent the semester working hard to "hit for the cycle" (a baseball term where a player gets a single, double, triple, and home run in the same game). He said that eighth grade was his last chance to do this before grades would count for admission to college and that he had worked hard to figure out how well to perform in each class to get the right grades for him (not us). We didn't much care about his intentions and dreams in this situation—we wanted performance!

Leaders can serve the important function of holding up a metaphorical mirror to help employees see how their behaviors are perceived by others. Formal 360-degree feedback assessments help employees learn how others perceive them on a set of leadership dimensions. Performance standards, quality reviews, and comments from others can help round out employees' self-perceptions.

Leaders may also help employees ascertain their identity by asking them to complete a time log and analyze the results. When we coach leaders, we often ask them to take the calendar test—to reflect on the last 90 days and consider:

- What categories of activities make up your workday?
- What issues have you spent the most time on?
- Whom have you spent the most time with?
- Where did you spend your time (in your office, in meetings, with customers)?
- What reports and information do you spend time looking at?
- What business issues capture your quiet time (keep you awake at night, float up when you are going to and/or from work, or surface often in conversations)?

As a leader, you should also be attuned to informal observations of your employees. Which employees tend to speak up first? Which employees have ideas that others follow? Which employees are listened to the most? Which employees are more bold, engaging, or creative? Which employees volunteer (or shy away from) certain assignments? Who does quiet service? Who works to engage others? As you thought-fully observe employees, you can begin to see patterns that reflect each employee's identity.

Collectively, these observations reveal predispositions, strengths, and weaknesses that form an identity pattern, helping leaders know how to engage the hearts, not just the hands and heads, of their team.

Conversations

Leaders may not think much about conversations they have with employees, but these conversations are often extremely potent for employees. Some of these conversations occur in formal performance review settings, where you evaluate productivity and potential. Often more crucial conversations occur when you quietly share your observations with employees. Some of these conversations may be about negative behaviors; others are about positive ones.

Child behavior experts find that punishing conversations make children fearful or angry but do little to change children's behavior. Much more effective are parents who frequently and warmly pay attention to and point out behavior that is appreciated and appropriate and pay minimal attention to problems. Discipline works best when a privilege is withheld briefly from a child with minimal display of parental emotion or engagement. The most effective parents reserve attention (and negative attention is still attention) for behavior they want to see more of.

Leaders do well to follow a similar pattern, commenting on, praising, and rewarding constructive work behavior and mostly ignoring annoyances. When a serious problem must be corrected, it is best to do so with minimal engagement by withholding pay or privileges, not engaging in yelling matches or protracted threats or shaming, all of which build resentment, not change.

Identity-clarifying conversations will focus less on judgment and more on description. As a leader, you might ask your employees to share their perceptions of their strengths, describe times when they demonstrated their strengths, and explore how their strengths might be used to help others (including coworkers and customers). You can describe what you see and value in their behavior, the effect it has on others for the good, and additional options for building on strengths.

Other strength-identifying conversations might occur in a team setting. More and more work is performed by teams that bring differing skills to common problems. (See Chapter 5.) A valuable team exercise is to ask team members to describe examples of the strengths of each individual on the team. This affirming report generally results in team members bonding more tightly with each other.

Assignments

We learn by doing. When we perform familiar tasks, we demonstrate our skills and take pleasure in our expertise. When we act outside of our comfort zone, we may learn hidden strengths we did not know we had. At other times we may learn that what we had hoped would be our strengths are actually not (e.g., Dave's short-lived basketball career). When we ask people how they learned what they care about and are good at, they realize that this insight has often emerged from tackling assignments both in and out of their comfort zone.

All talent management begins with hiring people who have the right strengths for the job, and these "right strengths" are customer defined. An executive once elaborated to Dave

..ow committed he was to managing people, to paying attention to their needs, and to helping them feel connected to the organization. He was a bit surprised when Dave suggested that helping his employees be happy was only the beginning point—hiring the right employees in the first place was another part of the journey. Such hiring is based on a simple criterion, not easily implemented: Are you hiring employees your customers would want you to hire? Are you the employer-of-choice of employees your customers would employ? Apple customers expect innovative design in their Apple products and service. Apple leaders need to make sure that new employees have creativity strengths and identity.

We don't always have the luxury of hiring the perfect employee or working at the best-fit job, however. We don't believe we have to start with a perfect fit in all cases or that we need to fire anyone whose signature strengths are not optimally aligned with corporate goals. For example, Raghu tended to be more comfortable in follower roles. His company was expanding and needed new leaders familiar with their customers and goals. They saw leadership potential in Raghu that he did not see himself. His manager began to assign him increasingly responsible leadership roles. He nervously accepted each assignment and did his best. Over time he recognized and developed his strengths as a leader and found great satisfaction and personal meaning in his new skills. He made valuable contributions to his company's emerging success.

Human resource systems like training and compensation may be used to help employees recognize and expand their strengths. Training opportunities provide forums to learn and apply new ideas, and pay programs may reinforce using those strengths.

As you help your employees recognize their identity and structure their work to build on strengths, don't ignore weaknesses. Building on strengths alone will not create leadership success. Dave hates to stretch, and Wendy hates to work up a sweat, but neither of us will be in great shape if we do only the physical activities that come naturally to us while ignoring all others. By helping employees recognize and face weaknesses, you also help them look honestly in the personal mirror and build an overall improvement process. As an identity builder, you offer employees a truer sense of self.

2. Define and Build Organizational Capabilities Required for Success

How does a leader define an organization's strengths, or capabilities? Think about two restaurants, computer stores, sports venues, hair salons, or other companies you have visited. While two companies in the same industry might offer similar products or services, can you sense a difference in how the companies work? These differences reflect an organization's identity. Disney theme parks create an entire world of whimsy and entertainment while Magic Mountain gives customers daring rides. Shopping at a local hardware store is different from buying hardware tools at Costco or Carrefour. A deli in New York feels different from a bistro in Paris. Organizations have an identity. Just as an individual's identity is shaped by his or her strengths, an organization's identity emerges from its capabilities.

Capabilities represent what the organization is known for, what it is good at doing, and how it patterns activities to deliver value. These capabilities include many of the intangible assets that investors pay attention to, the firm brand to which customers can relate, and the culture that shapes employee behavior. These capabilities also become the identity of the firm, the deliverables of HR practices, and the keys to implementing business strategy. An organization's capabilities are rooted in its values and reflect its reputation or brand.

We have generated a list of capabilities an organization might have and examples of companies that demonstrate them, shown in Table 3.1. It is not hard to see that the individual strengths listed in Figures 3.2 and 3.3 can also show up in corporate identities. Within an organization, pockets of functional expertise may need different strengths. Your leadership challenge is to align capabilities with strategies, evolve capabilities, and make sure management actions reinforce key capabilities.

Abundant organizations not only help individuals deploy and use their personal identity—they shape organizations with a clear identity. When those who work in the organization bring their different skills to bear on a common problem, there is diversity with unity. These organizations avoid groupthink by valuing different perspectives and strengths, but also they coalesce individual interests into shared organizational goals.

As a leader, you can commission capability audits to determine which of the capabilities are most critical to your organization's reaching its goals. For example, consumer product firms thrive on product innovation. These firms need to replace old products with new and improved ones in a timely way. Firms in more cost-competitive industries like retail need to build their efficiency capabilities. Walmart's

TABLE **3.1** Organization Capability Examples

PRINCIPLE *(What we are good at or known for)*	CAPABILITY *(What we do well in this domain)*	EXEMPLARY COMPANIES
TALENT Assuring competent and committed people	Attract, motivate, retain, and engage competent employees	Microsoft, Google
SPEED Making important changes happen fast	Change quickly to align with customer needs	Sony
SHARED MIND-SET Turning customer expectations into employee actions	Build a culture that reflects customer expectations and turns them into employee actions	Nokia
ACCOUNTABILITY Implementing discipline that results in consistent performance	Meet commitments and keep promises	FedEx
COLLABORATION Working across boundaries to ensure leverage and efficiency	Make the whole more than the sum of the parts	Disney
LEARNING Generating and generalizing ideas with impact	Generate new ideas and then generalize those ideas across boundaries	Accenture
LEADERSHIP BRAND Embedding leaders throughout the organization who embody the leadership brand	Identify a leadership brand that connects reputation with customers to employee behaviors	General Electric
INNOVATION Doing something new in both content and process	Innovate and create new ways to do things	Apple
STRATEGIC CLARITY Articulating and sharing a point of view about the future	Envision a future state and ensure that employees and practices are aligned to it	Nike
EFFICIENCY Managing the costs of operation	Increase efficiencies of scale and reduce costs	Walmart

continued

TABLE 3.1 Organization Capability Examples *(continued)*

PRINCIPLE *(What we are good at or known for)*	CAPABILITY *(What we do well in this domain)*	EXEMPLARY COMPANIES
SOCIAL RESPONSIBILITY Doing work that delivers value to society	Contribute to broader societal goals	British Petroleum
SIMPLICITY Making sure work is done as simply and efficiently as possible	Remove redundancies, reengineer processes, and accomplish work with fewer steps	Toyota or ConAgra
RISK MANAGEMENT Assessing the pros, cons, and probabilities associated with our work	Conduct regular and thorough risk analyses	Goldman Sachs

promise "always low prices" creates an identity in the mind of its customer but also guides its discipline in sourcing products, managing people, and building facilities.

When employees, customers, investors, and other stakeholders know what the organization is known for and good at doing, these capabilities build trust that the organization has enough and to spare to accomplish its purposes.

3. Meld Personal Strengths and Organizational Capabilities

How do leaders meld personal and organizational identity?

One of your leadership tasks is to help employees know whether and how they fit into the company. Sometimes fit or misfit is easy to define. The Federal Aviation Administration (FAA) is very clear that some people are more suited as air traffic controllers than others. Physical abilities (e.g., not being dyslexic) are prerequisites of course, but just as important (and harder to ascertain) are the strengths of managing stress, following detailed procedures, and remaining calm in a crisis. When the FAA started to source future air traffic controllers with police or military backgrounds (already practiced in these strengths), their retention and proficiency rates went up.

Disney theme parks communicate an identity. Their family-friendly, clean, and responsive image is upheld by employees around the globe who look and act in a particular way. They are less interested in creativity than in customer care, and they want employees who will play a role, enjoy the look of delight on a child's face, and handle repeated questions with courtesy—not merely work a register efficiently.

As a leader, you meld organization and personal identities by hiring, training, and compensating employees whose personal identity melds with the identity of the organization or its subparts. People find a sense of meaning, even abundance, when they are in an organization where they fit and feel valued for doing exactly what they do well. Leaders who are thoughtful about bringing in people who fit both technically and culturally help people find an abundant work setting.

In other cases, leaders meld personal and organization identity by shaping an individual's personal strengths into organization capabilities. The U.S. military acknowledges that it may not entice a lot of valedictorians as raw recruits. But the military is renowned for taking ordinary people and making them extraordinarily effective. Consistent and focused training and communication can change identities and shape how individuals respond to their situation.

Socialization of employees may begin on the first day of the job. As a new Ph.D. student, Dave was encouraged to attend faculty colloquiums where visitors would present their research and ideas. These seminars were seldom passive. Colleagues would push, prod, and challenge the work of the visitors to test the rigor and integrity of their ideas. By modeling to new Ph.D. students the importance of challenging ideas in a collegial setting, his faculty advisers mentored him into the role of a scholar scientist. They also learned which students would savor these inevitable clashes of ideas and which would run away. In contrast, Wendy's program was designed to train her as a psychologist. It focused on the student's willingness to look honestly at her own inner life with self-awareness and insight as a preparation for helping clients do the same.

As a leader, you may socialize employees through formal orientation programs where employees learn what is expected of them, but also through informal mentoring and coaching about unwritten rules and expectations for things like how to dress, how to show respect for others, how to deal with conflict, and what protocols govern decision making.

Go to dinner at your neighbor's. What are their routines? Who sits where? How is food passed? Does anyone say grace? (If so, who?) How are people dressed? How is the table set? Who cooks? Serves the food? Sits where? Who does dishes? Something as simple as having dinner at a friend's house demonstrates the many ways that two groups can differ in how they function. Fitting into someone else's family or work team or industry is seldom straightforward. In organizations with layers of complexity in history, rules, hierarchy, and routines, the job of helping others fit is much more difficult than serving a meal. But, when employees match their personal identity with the organization's identity, they are more able to use their strengths and to find meaning through work.

4. Determine Customer and Investor Expectations

How do leaders segment targeted customers and investors and determine their expectations?

Customer (and investor) segmentation means that not all customers or investors are equal. Companies who try to be all things to all customers generally serve none of them well. Segmenting customers means figuring out who are the target customers, those individuals or companies who will be critical to your future success. Segmentation may occur by product features, channel, desired service, or other features. Old Navy captured the essence of their targeted customer by putting a name on their prototype customer (Jenny), then making sure that employees throughout the organization know who "Jenny" was, what she wanted, and how best to serve her. Sharing customer information or creating a pseudo-customer helps employees know why they are in business and who they have to serve.

Once target customers are identified, leaders need to determine their buying criteria. Customers may pick suppliers based on price, service, quality, features, distribution, or brand. When leaders have a clear customer value proposition, they are able to enlist employees to meet those needs.

The same logic applies to investors. Figuring out who the investors are and their criteria for investing (e.g., growth versus value) helps leaders shape an organization agenda that meets those requirements.

5. Connect Both Personal and Organizational Identities with the Needs of Customers and Investors

How does a leader make sure that the fit between the individual and the organization also fits with customers and investors?

Fit for service does not just mean that individuals work well within their organizations but that there is a match between the employee inside and the organization's stakeholders outside. In the management literature the mantra "build on your strengths" has gained quite a bit of attention. When leaders help individuals shape their identity, clarify the organization's capabilities, and match individual strengths with organization capabilities, employees build on their strengths. But fully leveraging those strengths requires using those strengths to strengthen or serve others.

The movie *The Bucket List* reports the ancient Egyptian belief that the gatekeepers of heaven ask new arrivals two questions about their lives on earth: (1) Did you find joy in life? (2) Did your life bring joy to others? The first question is about building on your strengths—necessary but not sufficient. The second question shifts the focus of joy to helping others find it—building our strengths that strengthen others.

We can see the importance of turning personal strengths into value for others with a personal example. In college, Dave majored in English and developed a knack for reading novels. Even today, he can read two or three novels a week— what a strength! But few people care about his novel-reading strength. He can't make much of a living exercising this strength. His strength doesn't bring joy to anyone but himself. What others want from Dave is his ability to analyze a situation in ways that help them reach their goals (not his). Reading and interpreting good writing is a sustainable strength when it informs his ability to diagnose and help others work through their problems.

Great companies are not built on the great strengths of their leaders or employees but on how those strengths build value for their customers. To turn personal and organizational strengths into value for others:

Step 1: Be Clear About What You Want Your Organization to Be Known for by Your Best Customers. As stated earlier, an organization has an identity that becomes its firm brand, or reputation among customers. As a leader, you should make sure your top team and other employees have the same perception of what you want to be known for as an organization by your customers. A simple exercise is to have all members of your team write down three things they want your organization to be known for by its best customers in the future. Cluster these answers by themes and then see what percentage of the answers coalesce into the top three categories. Ideally at least 80 percent of the answers will fall into these top three clusters. For example, if there are 15 members of your team, you have 45 total answers. If 30 of these answers fall into the top three clusters of answers, you have a 67 percent shared identity. Repeat the exercise until you get close to 80 percent shared identity, which means your team has a shared view of what you want to be known for by your customers. In Table 3.1, we conclude from their brand identity and reputation that Apple wants to be known for innovation, British Petroleum for social responsibility, and Walmart for efficient production.

Step 2: Check It Out with Key Customers. Validate your identity or firm brand with key customers. Does the identity you claim cause customers to buy more from you? Apple's "innovative design" brand gets customers to pay a premium for the company's smart phones. Disney's "family entertainment" brings people long distances to experience Disney theme parks. Make sure that what you want to be known for is what your target customer cares about. A telecommunication company that pledged that customers would be able to hear a pin drop over their phone lines found that most customers didn't care much about pins dropping as long as their calls were not dropped.

Step 3: Make Sure That Organization Practices Inside Match the Intended Brand or Identity. When the identity you are known for by customers is reflected in practices inside your company, employees have a line of sight between their daily work and future customer value. We have found four actions that weave external identity into internal action.

First, leadership behaviors should be consistent with what the company as a whole is trying to communicate to customers. We call this *leadership brand*. Employees should be able to recognize in their leaders' actions the customer needs they are trying to meet. Leaders at Apple will act to encourage innovation and design, while leaders at Walmart will work to reduce costs and drive efficiency.

Second, craft top-down and across-the-aisle communication to share with everyone what you are trying to do. Repeat your desired identity over and over in speeches, workshops, and informal discussions, and capture it in symbols, slogans, logos, and advertisements. Never forget that behavior will communicate more convincingly than words and logos.

Third, encourage bottom-up problem solving where employees make the brand real to them. A wise leader once said, "I teach people correct principles and let them govern themselves." Leaders set direction top down but enlist action from the bottom up. This could mean involving employees in town hall meetings about problems, letting them act on challenges in real time, or building rapid-response teams. Make sure employees are clear about the principles that should guide their self-governance and problem-solving options. Such principles will emerge from the corporate identity you are trying to foster among your best customers.

Fourth, upgrade internal processes to institutionalize customer expectations. Processes may include how your organization turns customer insights into products, allocates money, pays people, or develops talent.

These steps are simple but not easy. They require leaders to identify the organization's key strengths (capabilities) and use them consciously to connect with targeted customers. But when this happens, individual employees see better how their work makes a difference for real people. There is a line of sight between what they do on Monday morning and who gets helped on Tuesday afternoon. Working from their strengths, they know they have enough skills and to spare to get the job done right. Connected with their values, they have a sense of contributing something they care about. Grounded in their character traits and virtues, they feel their own goodness in operation. This is abundance in action.

Summary: Leadership Actions to Build an Identity
○ Help employees become more aware of their signature strengths through assessment, conversation, observation, and assignment.

79

- ○ Define your organization's required strengths (or capabilities) by doing a capability audit.
- ○ Make sure that employees' strengths serve the organizational capabilities they are hired to build.
- ○ Define your key customers and investors and determine their expectations of you.
- ○ Connect the identity of the individuals and organizations to the customers they serve, building on strengths that strengthen others.

CHAPTER 4

Where Am I Going?
(Purpose and Motivation)

LEADERSHIP **PURPOSE** CHALLENGE

In a world of information overload and centrifugal goals, employees and organizations often spin away from their basic sense of purpose and direction. Great leaders recognize what motivates employees, match employee motivators to organization purposes, and help employees prioritize work that matters most.

ost in Wonderland, Alice approaches the grinning Cheshire cat to ask directions. When the cat asks where she is trying to go, Alice isn't quite sure. The cat provocatively states the obvious: it doesn't matter which road Alice takes if she doesn't know where she wants to end up.

Clarity about where we want to go and why is crucial to a sense of meaning and abundance. Where are we headed? What do we live for? Why do we do what we do? In the last chapter we looked at what we want to be known for—the strengths and personal values that become our hallmark. In this chapter we look at how leaders identify the end results that help us know which way to turn and motivate us to keep traveling.

Of course, the destinations we refer to are not found on maps. They are about the visions that call to us, the laurel wreaths that appeal to us, the relationships that matter to us, and the ideas that enthrall us. They are about our values, our desires, and the needs of humanity at large. One person's motivating destination is Olympic gold, while another's is gold in the bank. One person envisions a renewable planet; another values most a shining friendship and another an enlightening idea. Ultimately the abundant life seems to call us to the impossible—traveling toward many such destinations at the same time.

In this chapter we will explore how leaders establish a sense of direction or purpose that contributes to meaning inherent in the abundant organization.

Places to Go: Four Categories of Purpose

We propose four categories of destinations to help employees find meaning in good times or bad. These categories build on work by Frankl and others. (See Figure 4.1.) Leaders with a clear sense of these four categories are better prepared to establish a compelling vision with a clear line of sight between the work and the world that receives the work, set and accomplish goals that add value across multiple scorecards, and articulate ideas that preserve the learning of the past and imagine solutions for the future.

FIGURE 4.1 Types of Individual Purposes or Motivation

	Focus on Relationships	
Focus on Accomplishment	2 Achievement	4 Empowerment
	1 Insight	3 Connection

We will come back to these leadership agendas later; first let's examine the four categories they are built on in more detail.

Two dimensions characterize these categories: a low or high focus on accomplishment and a low or high focus on relationships with people. The resulting four categories are independent, so an individual can ultimately be low or high in each of the four categories independent of the others. Every category also embodies opportunities for either abundant, meaningful living or self-serving, unfulfilling existence. These four categories apply as much in Mumbai as they do in Paris or Sao Paolo. Let's flesh out these four categories.

1. Insight

On the bottom left is *insight*. This category represents low interest in either external accomplishment or relationships with other people, but potentially high interest in self-awareness, the life of the mind, the world of ideas, or personal experience for its own sake. We might think of a monk meditating quietly in a cave, a camper enjoying a mountain hike, or a thoughtful student examining inner motivations and feelings. At its best, insight promotes awareness, thoughtfulness, creativity, and deep appreciation for what is good in this moment. This person looks at a baby's first smile and thinks, "Look at that! I wonder what is going on in that little mind of his."

There are also low-abundance versions of insight. At a less abundant level we might imagine a hermit who has withdrawn into a highly personalized but redundant world, a depressed individual ruminating over his inadequacies, or a couch potato in front of a television set. Low-abundance employees may drift through the halls of the workplace with little sense of passion for their work, doing the minimum, staying under the radar, going through motions with little sense of self-efficacy or even desire.

The movie *A Beautiful Mind* portrays a range of possibilities from this quadrant. In this film an extremely intelligent and creative professor develops groundbreaking mathematical formulas and theories but also wrestles with the demon of schizophrenia and must fight against delusions and paranoia. At his worst, this individual becomes lost in the idiosyncratic world of his illness. At his best he becomes a Nobel Prize winner whose passion for his theories and formulas sparks creativity and insight in others.

People motivated by insight might find deep meaning in the world of ideas, in creating theories about themselves or the world, or in being mindful, present, and aware of their moment-by-moment experience. They know instinctively that self-awareness is the ultimate virtue. In this category we remember that all we really have is the present moment and that in that precise moment even great suffering can be bearable. Those who value insight find beauty or wonder in small details, exciting connections, or hopeful realizations.

In an organizational setting, individuals highly motivated by insight may provide thoughtful reflection on problems or opportunities. They may be involved in research and development—the search for new and creative solutions to old problems. They may provide the symbols, models, and connective images that capture people's imaginations and communicate powerfully. They are often motivated by the inherent value of a good idea and appreciate time to think and reflect. They remind us to appreciate the moment, learn from the past, or imagine the future. When things go wrong, their first instinct may be to say "Let's stop and think so that we can learn." Socially responsible individuals acting out of this quadrant focus on the data that shows the misuse and decline of the earth's resources. They write articles, give talks, and suggest policies that reflect the importance of sustainability.

Organizations motivated primarily by insight may include religious, philosophical, educational, or research institutions; yoga studios, cruise lines, or recreational facilities; museums, theaters, or national parks. They include industries focused on leisure arts, self-awareness, education, and self-improvement.

Not every organization will find its primary mission in the world of ideas. But every organization needs the abundance that comes from insight.

As a leader, consider where in your organization insight comes from: Who are the proponents of organizational self-reflection, self-awareness, and self-improvement? Who has new ideas, makes new connections, or comes up with suggestions for new ways to do business? Who creates the symbols that will inspire and instruct? Who stops to relish the moment and reminds others to do the same? Who remembers to honor the past? Who can imagine the future? Is the role of insight understood, valued, and promoted?

2. Achievement

On the top left is *achievement*. In this category are individuals who find meaning and purpose in doing, accomplishing, or just checking things off the list for the day. This quadrant is about getting something done and may include activities that are highly competitive or that require risk taking, discipline, and resilience in the face of failure. High-abundance members of the achievement group might include an athlete in training, an artist perfecting a painting, or a corporate executive planning an aggressive growth strategy for the company. Someone motivated by achievement looks at a baby's first smile and thinks, "How amazing! I wonder if she is developmentally on target for smiling."

Not all high-accomplishment activities are abundant with meaning. When achievement is devoid of moral values or becomes an end in itself, it may be characterized by ruthlessness, even cruelty. The TV show "The Apprentice," in which individuals compete in various business settings, suggests a high focus on achievement that becomes self-serving and callous. In the show competitors blame others for failures, see extravagance as the ultimate reward, and fear the boss's condemning words, "You're fired." Such an approach assumes that there is not enough to go around and that one person can win only when someone else loses. The deficit-oriented culture of "The Apprentice" dominates many corporations today.

In contrast, *Chariots of Fire* is a movie about British athletes in the 1924 Olympic games, all motivated to excel at their sports. One of the athletes is discouraged from competing by his sister because she sees no value in sports and believes his destiny is to be a Christian missionary in China. He responds, "I believe God made me for a purpose—for China. But He also made me fast. And when I run, I feel his pleasure." People motivated by achievement love to accomplish for the sake of accomplishment. Corporations in which achievement takes abundant forms are among the most successful and admired of companies.

People motivated by achievement might find meaning in simply getting things done and in winning. They generally enjoy improving and may strongly identify with their skills and accomplishments. Thus they like setting and meeting goals, getting feedback and having clear scorecards for measuring success, and being recognized for their accomplishments. They want measurable action plans that track results. In this category failure is an impetus for learning and there is always room to improve. These folks know instinctively that unless the organization provides real value and succeeds economically it simply won't survive.

In an organizational setting, individuals highly motivated by achievement are generally hardworking and internally motivated. They often provide energy and drive to get the job done. They may flourish in competitive environments but are not necessarily trying to best others as much as solve problems and improve their own performance. Whether they are the rough carpenters who love getting the framework in quickly or fine craftsmen who relish detail work and fine finishes, people motivated by achievement take satisfaction in wielding their craft in ways others will respect. When things go wrong, their first instinct may be to ask, "What can we learn? How can we improve?"

Organizations motivated by achievement may focus on technology, sports, or the arts, but they will not just be along for a pleasant ride. They will be at the cutting edge, pushing the envelope of skill or design. They include industries focused on scientific progress, high return on investment, competition, or excellence in any domain. They may especially value high returns or good marketing but will get the biggest charge out of being among the best at what they do. "Winning" is their mantra, goal, and passion, and they write about and savor their triumphs and successes.

Not every organization will care to compete at the highest level. But every organization can benefit from the abundance that comes from achievement.

In your organization, where does achievement occur? Who are the proponents of achievement who push for learning and want to get better and better? Is achievement fostered by tailoring challenging assignments, providing clear feedback on performance (preferably with ways to actually count success or improvement), and recognizing improvement and success?

3. Connection

On the bottom right is *connection*, which is characterized by less focus on achievement and higher focus on relationships. People in this category find meaning in life through people they meet and interact with. Some will be energized by a few intimate relationships, others by looser ties with many people, but the common thread will be satisfaction and meaning through relating to others. This person looks at a baby's first smile and thinks, "Oh, he likes me! Now we have a relationship."

Again, there are low-abundance and high-abundance versions of this category. Lower-abundance versions might be people who are interpersonally needy or codependent or who like parties and social events but don't develop real relationships of mutual trust, understanding, or care. These workers hang around at the watercooler but may be more invested in gossip or being liked than in getting the job done.

A higher-abundance version of connection might be a devoted parent, a trusted friend, or a skilled networker. Connectors find deep meaning in sharing life with other people, and people are the priority that gives meaning to everything else in their lives. At its best, connection motivates peace making, compassion, cooperation, and teamwork and fosters skill in listening, empathy, honesty, and service. Socially responsible connectors form advocacy groups, lobby for change, and rally support for environmental activism.

In an organizational setting, individuals highly motivated by connection grease the skids to help people get along at work. They consider the impact decisions will have on real people. They tune in to the needs and feelings of customers. They may have good intuition for solving interpersonal problems or creating systems to coordinate efforts of diverse groups. Under dire conditions, they endure so they can be reunited with or help those they love. They know instinctively that people matter more than things, more than policies, more than money, more than anything.

Organizations motivated by connection may include service-oriented industries of all kinds, clubs and sports leagues, neighborhood or civic groups, the social arm of religious groups, and extended family structures. They include industries focused on helping people meet, mediating conflicts, supporting families, and socializing the rising generation. Within companies human resource departments are often charged with concern for connection needs.

Not every organization finds its primary mission in getting people together. But every organization benefits from the abundance that comes from connection.

In your organization, where does connection live? Who are the proponents of people-oriented policies and programs? Whether or not your organization is explicitly service oriented, who pays attention to the needs of people both inside the organization and as customers and stakeholders? Any organization that does not provide real value to real people is unlikely to endure over time.

4. Empowerment

On the top right is *empowerment*, characterized by a high need for achievement that is channeled into high investment in people, especially in working to overcome human suffering. A high-abundance version of empowerment would be the TV show "Extreme Makeover: Home Edition," where skilled designers and craftsmen use their talents and skills to redesign and rebuild an unworkable house for a deserving but impoverished family. They tailor the new house to the needs and personalities of the family, involving the whole community and working against the clock to finish the house in a week. The needs, feelings, and desires of people are foremost in such scenarios, but so are the skills, learning, and accomplishments of those who try to help. Other examples might be a skilled teacher who loves developing students, a talented political leader who finds creative solutions to real-world problems, and a hardworking religious leader who loves using her skills to empower others. An individual motivated by empowerment sees a baby's first smile and thinks, "This is the hope of the future. Children will change the world."

A low-abundance version of empowerment might involve overpowering others and attempting to enforce one's will through intimidation or force. Even if real problems are being addressed, the focus would not be on empowering others but on self-aggrandizement or personal ambition. Low-abundance employees who are motivated by empowerment may be dominating or demanding, more interested in garnering power than in sharing it.

People motivated by the abundant version of empowerment might find deep meaning in social responsibility pursuits like finding a cure, reducing world hunger, or freeing political prisoners. They may also find great meaning in cleaning up a local park, serving food at a homeless shelter, or teaching a child to read. *Empowerment* may motivate someone to run for political office, become a high school teacher, or take over the lead of a troubled company. But high-abundance empowerment is not about accruing power over others; rather it is about helping others find their own voice, options, and personal clout.

In an organizational setting, individuals highly motivated by empowerment often gravitate to management/leadership or coaching/teaching positions. They like to see others succeed and want to make a difference for good. They may be good mentors, may be motivated to produce products that address a pressing problem, or may lead in charitable campaigns and community service.

Organizations motivated by empowerment may include political parties, nongovernment organizations, penal institutions, news agencies, volunteer groups, charitable organizations, or educational institutions emphasizing training and job skills. They include industries focused on medical advances and services, underserved populations, food production and distribution, ecology, energy production, and family services. Empowerment reminds us that suffering is unavoidable but that we can choose our attitude and response to suffering. We can ignore it, blame others, or give up in despair . . . or respond to it from our deepest values of compassion and courage. Empowerment is a powerful antidote to the societal plagues of isolation, despair, and ennui.

Not every organization will find its primary mission in humanitarian service. But every organization can benefit from a value proposition grounded in empowerment.

In your organization, where does empowerment percolate? Who are the proponents of social responsibility? Who helps everyone understand how his or her work is connected to the greater good and the needs of real people? Is there a clear line of sight between today's work and the world's problems?

Self-Awareness for Leaders, Employees, and Organizations

These four categories suggest four destinations that motivate people and bring meaning to life. As a leader, you can bring these motivating purposes into your organization at four levels.

First, know yourself. Know which of the four destinations or quadrants is motivating to you personally, be familiar with how these motivations may have changed over your lifetime, and look for ways to expand your repertoire to include elements of all the quadrants.

Second, know your employees. You can help employees in your part of the organization to identify the destinations or quadrants that are most motivating to them, helping them make sure the work they do ties into that motivation. Placing insight-driven employees into achievement positions or tasks will both frustrate the individual and limit the quality of work done.

Third, know your organization. You can help define for your part of the organization the motivations most relevant to your work. You can also articulate for others how each of the four quadrants contributes to bringing meaning, direction, and motivation to work.

Fourth, position your organization to have a socially responsible agenda. You can connect individual goals to broader societal goals through philanthropy and giving programs (be a company with a caring heart), through social activism (monitor and control use of carbon and other resources), and through work/life policies (offer employees control and flexibility for their work).

To identify what motivates you, your employees, and your organization, we highly recommend the following exercise (even if insight is not your strong suit):

PART 1
- For 20 minutes, write whatever comes to mind describing what your life would look like five years from today if you had become your best self and all your dreams were realized.
- For an additional 20 minutes, write whatever comes to mind describing what your organization (or division) would look like five years from today if it had become the best it could be and all your dreams for it were realized.

Repeat this exercise tomorrow to give your thoughts time to percolate.

If you have *any* interest in trying this exercise, which we hope you will, please do not read further until you do at least one of these writing exercises. You will glean a lot more information from Part 2 below if you do Part 1 first.

Psychologist David McClelland analyzed writing samples for evidences of what motivates human beings. He found that the needs for achievement, connection, and power showed up repeatedly in what people wrote, providing the basis for his theories about human motivation. While we won't try to be that scientific here, take a moment to look at the scenarios you created in this exercise.

PART 2

○ Looking through what you wrote, put an *I* for *insight* in the margin for any words from your success scenario that refer to creativity, imagination, symbols, self-awareness, balance, thoughtfulness, thinking for thinking's sake, or having great ideas.

○ Put an *A* for *achievement* in the margin for any words that refer to setting or achieving goals, learning so as to improve, developing skills, exercising resilience to keep trying at a difficult task, or gaining recognition for accomplishments.

○ Put a *C* for *connection* in the margin for words referring to good relationships with others, spending time with people, meeting people or bringing people together, deepening relationships, feelings of mutual care and support, or being with people you love.

○ Put an *E* for *empowerment* in the margin for words referring to solving world problems, making a difference, mentoring or developing others, seeing people succeed, providing resources or services to others, or gaining recognition for social responsibility.

    ○   Count up how many of each letter you have. And yes, you can count double for items that have high value to you or that you elaborate on.

Once you have used the exercise to identify the destinations you find most motivating to pursue, you will know more about the compelling whys that support the hows of your life. You can then deepen, expand, and focus to increase your sense of purpose and direction. You can help employees do the same. Let's explore these ideas further from a personal and leadership perspective.

Find the High-Abundance Version of Your Quadrant

As noted, each of these quadrants has low-abundance and high-abundance versions. The difference often is found in the moral values of the individual. Responding from our highest moral values tips the scales in favor of abundance. For example, think of a challenge you faced in the past that was extremely difficult for you—either at work, in your family, or in your personal life. As you think back on that challenge, what do you feel best about in terms of how you handled it? Are you most satisfied with how you kept your calm, showed honesty or authenticity, showed your sense of humor, forgave, learned from mistakes, or perhaps just kept going and didn't give up? If you had it to do over again, what would you do differently (in 10 words or less)? What personal values show up in your answers?

Now think about the most pressing challenges in your life right now. Consider finances, family, health, losses, business downturns, tough relationships, transitions, etc. Now think of yourself looking back on this challenge from the perspective of many years from now. As you look back, what would you want to feel good about in how you handled the current difficulty? What values are most important to you to maintain and live from? What do you care most about in terms of your personal integrity in this situation? These are the values that saturate the high-abundance versions of the four quadrants—values like integrity, gratitude, humility, kindness, discipline, and compassion.

Now think about the most pressing challenges you face as a leader at work. How can you apply your personal values to these leadership challenges, helping others apply their personal values to meeting these challenges? When people apply their personal values to pressing business challenges, both individuals and organizations are more apt to succeed.

Expand into Other Quadrants

Even though we concentrate our efforts in one quadrant or another to start, great leaders must have at least moderate proficiency in all four quadrants to motivate all types of employees and respond to all types of challenges. A good place to expand is into the quadrant on the opposite corner from the one you prefer. For example, if you work primarily in the achievement quadrant, consider bringing into your life a balancing experience with investing more in connection, spending time with people regardless of their usefulness. Or if you love empowerment, consider adding a component of insight to give yourself time for rest, self-reflection, and fresh ideas.

One of us (guess who!) feels very comfortable in the insight quadrant and loves the world of self-exploration and reflection. But she has learned over the years that the comfortable world of ideas is hard to justify unless she moves across the chart to the opposite corner—the world of empowerment, where ideas become real in the lives of other people. Unless she is writing, speaking, serving, and listening to the real problems of real people, her grand ideas quickly become sterile and boring. Other people's challenges challenge her to think differently about her own and push her to not only build on her strengths but also use them to strengthen others.

To some extent movement from one quadrant to another is a developmental process. We may need to concentrate our desires in one quadrant for a time, but over a lifetime can shift energy into new desires.

The other one of us (guess again!) majors in the quadrant of achievement, with a strong minor in insight. He spent many of his early professional years exploring exciting ideas, writing books, and developing a reputation as a thought leader in human resources and leadership. He loves crossing things off the daily to-do list and feels energized by his internal scorecard for accomplishments for the day. But in more recent years he is discovering the abundance that comes in investing more in family, friends, and community. Professionally he has moved more into both executive coaching and consulting with governments and international companies, trying to make a difference for good in people's lives.

Few people start out with motivation in all four quadrants. To raise a family a person might concentrate on relationships for a time, putting achievement needs on hold. Another may invest heavily in achievement in the early stages of a career and then become more motivated by insight and the need for self-reflection later on. As we become aware of the limits of the quadrant we have been in, we may feel regret, even guilt, about not having balanced our lives better. But every life involves compromises and trade-offs, and few of us have the energy to support all four quadrants equally at the same time, especially early in life. Over a lifetime we can expand our repertoire of motivations and desires to include all four quadrants, even if we will always lean toward one or two.

It has been said that the abundant life begins when we give up all hope of ever having a better past. Many of us do not realize that clinging to the hope of a better past keeps us from finding meaning and purpose today. We covertly act as though if we are frustrated and unhappy enough about our regrets somehow life will take pity on us and undo them. Facing this false hope for what it is and willingly relinquishing it opens up the time frame in which real hope lies: the present.

In a similar way, a company cannot afford to be motivated indefinitely by one quadrant at the expense of the other three. Social responsibility initiatives for protecting the environment or serving the underprivileged (empowerment) must be informed by thoughtfulness and awareness of our limitations (insight). Human capital and employee initiatives (connection) must be tempered with the need for profitability, market penetration, and capital investments (achievement). Different divisions or employees may be charged with championing the whys associated with a particular quadrant but must remember that cooperation is needed to ensure that all the quadrants are accounted for in the organization's overall structure and direction. Many European organizations measure their success by financial, customer/employee, and societal results—the so-called triple bottom line, often called the 3-Ps of performance, people, and planet. Corporate balanced scorecards help leaders match employees' desired destination with their organization position.

Find the Right Fit

Leaders need to help employees and organizations find a good fit between the purposes that motivate the individual and the purposes that motivate the business as a whole. The higher leaders are in the organization, the more broadly they need to think about the purposes or destinations the organization seeks and the more they need to "walk in four directions at once" while keeping a clear sense of their overall purpose.

Sylvia was a talented human resources manager with an Ivy League education and a passion for women's rights. She was hired in part because of her organization's commitment to equality. But when Sylvia's passion took over every aspect of her work to such an extent that she could talk of little else, her empowerment motivation ran amok, untempered by other business realities. While higher-ups valued her passion for equality, they also needed to attend to other purposes to keep the business profitable and contributing value for all of its constituents. Her single-focused why might have been a terrific fit in a government human rights agency, but it did not serve her (or others) well in her capacity as a business leader who needed to attend to all four quadrants.

While no organization will endure for long if it is not firmly grounded in empowerment agendas, ultimately the goal is to empower, serve, and create value for customers and stakeholders, not just to stroke the empowerment agendas of individual employees. Having said that, the more firmly grounded an organization is in the quadrant of empowerment—highly focused on both accomplishment and people—the more that organization can keep a clear line of sight between what it does well and the needs of customers.

A Leadership Agenda

While leaders need to walk in four directions at the same time, it is important to learn how to manage priorities and results across the four quadrants. Herbert Simon, the Nobel prize-winning economist defined the principle of satisficing. Satisficing suggests that some quadrants, though worth doing, may not be worth excelling at. There are things that are worth doing but worth doing poorly. Those quadrants that define our identity and purpose require our maximum efforts and energy. Like Kobe Bryant's commitment to winning basketball games, these will be the essence of our game, the desires and strengths we rely and build on for success. Other quadrants we will satisfice, meeting basic criteria so these things won't interfere with other goals rather than looking for the very best way to approach them. Like Bryant's jump shots, we need to do these things moderately well but not superbly. In a world of limited resources of time, funds, and energy, it is crucial to know the primary motivations and purposes to which we will give our best effort and the secondary motivations and purposes that we will make do on. Then we to make peace with the compromises we all must make about where we spend limited energy.

Leaders can bring direction and purpose to their organizations and employees by asking:

○ **What are the insights we need to succeed as an organization?** Who spends time thinking and reflecting on these insights? Who has responsibility for new ideas, learning from the past, and reflecting on our current situation? How do we make room for pondering, reflection, learning, and creativity?

○ **What achievements and goals will keep us in business?** Who spends time clarifying those goals, working toward their accomplishment on a daily basis, and acknowledging and rewarding their accomplishment? How do we promote efficiency and clarity to help people do their work with commitment and competence?

○ **What types of relationships will help us get our work done?** Who spends time investing in people, listening to their ideas, building congenial teams, caring about the individual, and keeping people connected? How do we build skills of communication, compassion, respect, and cooperation?

○ **What human problems are we trying to solve?** Who spends time creating a clear line of sight between what we do and what our customers, stakeholders, and the world at large need? Who makes sure employees understand how the work they do makes a difference for real people? How do we communicate our empowerment agenda to all?

o **Which are the most pressing motivations of this organization, and where do they fall among the four quadrants of insight, achievement, connection, and empowerment?** Which of the four quadrants will we excel at, and where will we satisfice?

It is easy to lose track of our primary motivations and where we are going in the rush of work, the complexity of the world, or the press of adversity. But when we start wondering what the point of all our labor is, remembering the whys that delineate our destinations helps us put up with the hows. In the words of Viktor Frankl:

> It did not really matter what we expected from life, but rather what life expected from us. We needed to stop asking about the meaning of life, and instead to think of ourselves as those who were being questioned by life—daily and hourly. Our answer must consist, not in talk and meditation, but in right action and in right conduct. Life ultimately means taking the responsibility to find the right answer to its problems and to fulfill the tasks which it constantly sets for each individual.

Summary: Leadership Actions to Articulate a Purpose

o Help employees recognize what motivates them (insight, achievement, connection, empowerment).
o Match the employees' motivation with the organization task they are assigned to perform.
o Create an organization aspiration that declares a socially responsible agenda and translates that agenda to individual action.
o Help employees satisfice in those tasks that are worth doing poorly and prioritize tasks that are important to do well.

CHAPTER 5

Whom Do I Travel With? (Relationships and Teams [Th]at Work)

LEADERSHIP **RELATIONSHIP** CHALLENGE

[
Despite increasingly competitive and isolating work settings and declining interpersonal skills, much work has to be accomplished with others and within teams. Great leaders help employees build skills for professional friendships between people and among teams.
]

Ask 10 people what brings them joy, and chances are good at least half will refer to people they love. One of the saddest experiences of Wendy's career was talking to a client who was extremely distraught by the 9/11 phone calls that a man on one of the hijacked planes made to say good-bye to his wife. She too was upset by this image, wondering what it would feel like to receive such a call. But that wasn't what had upset him. "You don't get it," he said. "What is so hard for me is that if I had been on that plane, I would have no one to call." It is hard to imagine abundance or meaning in life without people to share it with. Friendship helps not only our leisure time teem with abundance but our work teams as well.

While much of the joy in daily life comes from sharing it with others, the challenges of getting along have not diminished with all of our technology for connecting. In fact, the anonymity of e-mails, Tweets, Web-based bulletin boards, and blogs often intensifies the challenge as it removes the personal touch so central to meaningful relationships. Globalization and equal hiring initiatives mean more and more of us work with people of different cultures, backgrounds, orientations, races, and life stages. Increasingly complex work necessitates coordinating efforts among people of diverse professional training to bring products to fruition or provide the range of services expected. Getting along with people who differ from us in either overt or subtle ways requires skill, patience, self-awareness, curiosity, and empathy. And getting along with others is catching. When one person is happy, others share the joy, and vice versa. Students with more depressed roommates become more depressed, and students with more optimistic teachers become more positive.[1]

And yet we seem to have less and less opportunity to develop the very relational skills we need. Spending our days in front of screens and hooked into earphones reduces face-to-face contact and visual cues for reading one another, so we get less practice in real-time talking and listening. What we see on those screens increasingly involves gamesmanship, overt hostility, partisanship, backstabbing, and cutthroat competition, with few role models for healthy relating.

Fortunately, as we come to value the human element at work, some of the old rules about not fraternizing are starting to soften a bit. When research suggests that people with at least one really good friend at work are more apt to like their job and stick with it, friendship at work becomes an asset rather than a liability. Research by the Gallup Organization reveals that employees who have a best friend at work are *seven times* more likely to be highly engaged at work than those who do not. Those with a close friend at work are almost *twice* as likely to be satisfied with their pay, and that number stretches to *three* times as likely for those in the *lowest*-paying jobs. People with close friends at work are 27 percent more likely to see their strengths as aligned with the company's goals. These friendship claimers are also statistically more likely to satisfy customers, get more done in less time, have more fun on the job, have fewer accidents at work, innovate and share ideas more, and simply show up more consistently. Those with three or more close friends at work report even more increases in work and life satisfaction.[2] While work friendships can create problems as well, the advantages of having strong friendships and good relationships at work seem to far outweigh the disadvantages.

Effective leaders play an important role in helping subordinates make friends, build strong teams, resolve conflicts, get along with customers, and build relationships of trust, support, and *abundance* throughout the organization. Effective leaders also reap the benefits of personal engagement and satisfaction when they have close friends at work.

One plant manager who was worried about abysmal scores on employee engagement measures (along with high customer complaints, high absenteeism, a poor safety record, and low overall plant performance) decided she had little to lose by trying to foster friendship among her employees (who were all men, almost all over 40, and described as hard-nosed manufacturing line workers). She began talking about the importance of caring for each other, set up a social fund to give employees money for outings with coworkers and their families, kept communication open, and openly encouraged friendship among her employees. The attitude and feeling at work changed, people started having more fun at work, and the plant became simply a more pleasant place to be. These "soft" changes also translated into hard improvement in productivity and customer perceptions. A year later the employee engagement scores were up dramatically, as were productivity and plant safety. Customer complaints decreased 50 percent, and absenteeism dropped. These trends continued the following year.[3]

Just as good parents let their kids work out their friendship squabbles on their own if they can, effective leaders get out of the way of other people's relationships. But effective leaders also provide opportunities for people to get together, and they model good listening and sincere apologies, demonstrate caring, and when necessary help mediate problems. Relationships are too important to our sense of abundance and meaningful life to ignore. When people come together to make ideas grow, ideas improve and the people find more meaning. What's more, research like that just cited suggests that good work relationships mean good business.

A Relationship Playbook

What makes for good relationships at work? It is one thing to get along while we veg out in front of the TV with someone.

It is quite another to get along while designing a new Web page, coordinating efforts to clean up an oil spill, or hammering out the details of a merger. What are the keys to getting along while getting things done?

Historically, folk wisdom, family role models, and religious teachings have been humanity's primary sources of information about what makes relationships survive and thrive. In recent years, researchers have made relationships a scientific agenda, complete with video cameras, statistical analyses, and brain imaging techniques to help us understand the nitty-gritty of how people interact. We've sampled that literature with a simple question in mind: What are the most important skills that grease the skids of human connection? We looked for fundamentals, but fundamentals with a punch—with proven results, solid research, and sensible theory to back them up. We wanted the essential skills that will allow someone to play the relationship game with a reasonable chance of success, both so relationships can thrive and so work can get accomplished.

We've grouped our findings into five learnable skill sets that seem to capture much of what it takes to promote genuine connection. As individuals develop these skills, leaders emulate them, teams adopt them, and organizations foster them, the magic fairy dust of human connection can increasingly sprinkle down on the practical world of work. These five skill sets are:

1. Make and respond to bids
2. Listen and self-disclose
3. Navigate proximity
4. Resolve conflict
5. Make amends

Make and Respond to Bids

Irene felt lucky to land a job right out of college, even if it meant a move to a new area. While Irene anticipated an adjustment period, she was unprepared for the cool reception she received at her new job. She enjoyed her clients, but the other employees seemed preoccupied and distant. The secretary smiled vacantly and showed her the copy machine but had little to say. Staff meetings consisted of the office manager reading off policy changes or calendar events while everyone listened in polite boredom. Irene resented being expected to spend many uncompensated hours each week completing paperwork as part of a new initiative, but when she raised the issue in the staff meeting, the supervisor gave everyone a lecture about budget cuts and how lucky they were to have jobs. Irene needed the money, but she began to wonder about the "lucky" part.

Whether we are new to a company or have worked there for 20 years, the process of finding supportive relationships, building good teams, or making "best friends" at work begins with making and receiving "bids." Relationship expert John Gottman defines a bid as a request for attention.[4] A bid might be a smile or a touch, simply looking someone in the eye, saying hello, offering a compliment, sharing something personal, requesting help, or asking a question. In the world of relationships, nothing happens until someone makes a bid. At Irene's company the art of bidding had apparently been absorbed into the holes in the soundproofing tile: no one had much interest in anyone else at work.

Equally important in the bidding process is the response we get to our bids. If the other party does not respond by paying attention to our bid in a positive way, the game stops, like a ball that dies when a tennis serve is not returned.

Unlike the tennis serve, the goal of a bid is not to defeat the opponent but to encourage a volley. In fact, even in established relationships people are not very apt to keep bidding if we don't hit the ball back. Gottman's research found that an overt bid that is not responded to is almost never repeated. This suggests that it is just as important that we respond to other people's bids as that we make bids.

Both making and responding to other people's bids are crucial when we are new or when others are new to our organization. But even when people are established, relationships founder when no one is bidding or when bids are ignored. Even with old friends or family, unrequited bids are unlikely to be repeated. This doesn't mean we have to accept every lunch invitation or agree to help everyone who asks, but our response to these bids needs to acknowledge the bidder and give positive attention even if we can't go along. "I'm swamped" does little to grease the skids of emotional connection but will leave the bidder feeling exposed and ignored, where "Darn, wish I could. Could we reconnect in three weeks when this project is further along?" might save the volley. Even "I'm almost always committed for lunch, but have you thought of asking Tom?" might successfully redirect the ball to a more suitable player while keeping the bidder in the game.

When we raise concerns or work issues, we are also bidding for a kind of attention. The staff meetings in the preceding example were littered with the rejected bids of staff members whose concerns or questions had been virtually ignored. These dropped bids cluttered the emotional court of the staff meetings, resulting in employees who felt little commitment to the workplace, little involvement with one another, and little confidence in management.

109

Arina, a supervisor in a large social service agency, noticed that even though many of the employees were friendly and connected, others seemed to operate on the sidelines. Many of the latter were talented individuals whose work benefited the agency, but Arina felt like they were not having a great experience at work and wondered how long they would stay once other opportunities opened up. She took time during a training meeting to discuss the concept of bids, gave a playful demonstration of making and receiving bids, and invited discussion about what happens when bids are ignored. She encouraged everyone to pay more attention to both making and responding to bids and made sure she modeled the changes she was hoping for. She continued to bring up the concept of bids often, asked the less connected employees about their experience with bidding and responding to others' bids, and deliberately set up time for people to connect informally. The atmosphere at the agency began to warm up, and at least some of the folks she had worried about losing started to make better connections at work.

Think about a bid for attention you have made today. What did you do? How did the other person receive your bid? Did he or she keep the volley going? Who made a bid for your attention today? Did you return the serve or let the ball bounce off the court while you looked something up on the Internet or rushed to meet a deadline? We have encouraged people to set a goal of having at least one meaningful encounter with a person each day. While this sounds easy, it often requires consciously making and receiving bids rather than falling back into personal isolation.

How would you rate the confidence people in your organization feel to make and respond to bids? Do you make a point as a leader to greet and engage people in conversation, respond attentively to their bids, and encourage others to do the same? Or are too many balls dropping out of play, making the workplace feel cool and flat? Do people at all levels understand the importance of simply making and responding to bids?

Listen and Self-Disclose

Once a relationship has been opened by a bid, two simple skills help deepen the connection: good listening and appropriate self-disclosure. These are the skills that allow close friendships to develop out of mere acquaintances. And close friendships not only lead to more engagement and satisfaction at work; they lead to a sense of meaning or abundance.

While we often think our best friends are people we have a lot in common with, research suggests that proximity is really the more important variable in who will become a close friend. Our friends are more likely to be the people who live next door than the people who live just a block away, more likely to be people in our office than one building over, more likely to be people we sit next to in a class than those across the room. Sure, among the 150 or so people we interact with regularly we will often choose to get closer to those who like the things we like or who see the world as we see it, but in almost any group of 150 we can find such people with a little effort.

In addition to good eye contact and an open posture, many good listeners take the time to restate what they are hearing to make sure they understand both the content and the feelings involved. "Wait a minute; let me make sure I understand. So you think . . . Am I understanding that right? What am I missing?" This simple three-part formula communicates real listening:

1. I'm hearing . . .
2. Is that right?
3. Is there anything else?

This formula comes in especially handy when feelings are strained or emotions run high, but it is also valuable in any kind of negotiation, including the negotiation of a new relationship.

Of course, even the best of listeners won't get anywhere unless someone else talks. Work doesn't always feel like a safe place to disclose the things that keep us awake at night or that are at the core of our innermost feelings. Nor do we especially care to hear the details of everyone else's colonoscopy, marital discord, or high school basketball career. But people don't get the benefit of having close friends at work unless they are willing to take some risk in letting people know a little more about them than what is on their résumé. And that means work has to be a reasonably safe place for people to be honest.

Leaders can help create that sense of safety by listening carefully to others and restating others' opinions and feelings, especially when conflict or tension exists. They can also model appropriate self-disclosure by sharing their values and experiences from time to time, either one on one or in public. But self-disclosure without self-awareness or without being interested in others as well can backfire. If one person reveals too much too fast or too often while the other only listens, the "friendship" will feel more like therapy or parenting than genuine two-way connection.

Self-disclosure requires real self-awareness so one person does not dominate conversations or throw work meetings off track with too many personal stories. Everyone wants to know what the leader thinks, but only to a point. A leader who hijacks meetings with personal opinions, stories, or dramas will soon be resented by those who have no choice but to listen. Friendship is based on reciprocity, with roughly equal amounts of talking and listening on both sides and with roughly equal levels of self-disclosure. One relationship expert recommends setting a goal of three genuine connections each day. What would happen to our experience of personal abundance if we made a point to really connect in an honest and meaningful way at least three times every day?

To what extent do people who work together in teams or in your organization respectfully listen to each other at both a factual and a feeling level? Do people feel heard? Are leaders especially careful to listen, not just pontificate? Is it safe to say what is really on one's mind? Such an atmosphere helps foster the good listening and appropriate self-disclosure that fosters deeper friendships as well as healthy work environments.

Navigate Proximity

So what happens to work while all this love is being passed around? Fortunately for our pocketbooks, human beings need more than symbiotic clinging to one another to be happy. We not only want connection—sometimes we also want to be left alone. Linguist Deborah Tannen reminds us, "There is comfort in being understood and pain in the impossibility of being understood completely. But there is also comfort in being different—special and unique—and pain in being the same as everyone else, just another cog in the wheel."[5]

Relationships are always working at cross-purposes to some extent because people have conflicting needs for both involvement and individuality, time together and time apart. As our need for closeness is met, we begin to feel more keenly our need for solitude, for achievement, or for respite from the anxiety of relating. When we get too far into our own heads or work, we start to long for contact with others. But when we get too much of that good thing, we start to long for time apart. Tannen goes on to say, "It's a double bind because whatever we do to serve one need necessarily violates the other. . . . Because of this double bind, communication will never be perfect; we cannot reach stasis. We have no choice but to keep trying to balance independence and involvement, freedom and safety, the familiar and the strange—continually making adjustments as we list to one side or the other."[6]

In navigating these competing needs, Tannen finds that women in conversation often emphasize how people are alike, while men more readily point out differences.[7] When we don't play our expected gender role when talking with our own gender, we may create mistrust or confusion without anyone really knowing why. Likewise, when men and women talk together, they may wonder why they end up feeling at cross-purposes. Regardless of gender, our competing needs for solidarity and solitude, sameness and uniqueness are probably easier to balance if they are explicit to us and others.

Another aspect of closeness and distance is also important to consider in work relationships. To illustrate, ask yourself whom you would be most likely to turn to if you needed a creative solution to a problem—a close friend or a relative stranger. While we would probably feel more *comfortable* turning to a close friend, research by Mark Granovetter[8] suggests that we will probably get a more creative solution from the stranger. People we don't know as well are more likely to think of something we haven't thought of, to bring fresh perspectives and unusual information to bear on our problem.

For the introverts among us who see little value in "wasting time" networking or making small talk, this is a helpful insight. I may get more feel-good support from people I've known long and well, but I'm more likely to get unexpected approaches to old problems from people on the fringes of my comfort zone. These are folks who are less likely to already think like I do. Doris Kearns Goodwin determined that President Abraham Lincoln's political genius included his willingness to bring together a "team of rivals" to staff his cabinet—people who not only had *not* supported his presidency and his viewpoints but who were his major competitors.[9]

We don't need the complexity of trying to work with people who intensely dislike us to get the benefits of peripheral contacts, however. Jeff is a volunteer employment specialist in the church group we attend. Of the 100 or so families who attend our congregation, roughly 10 have lost jobs, another 10 need upgraded employment, and at least 10 more have seen real economic losses in their family businesses. Jeff decided to see if the members could help each other, so he opened his home on a Sunday evening meeting to everyone who wanted to come to share ideas for improving his or her work situation. The dozen people who showed up included a realtor who was thriving on foreclosures and wanted to help others, a colonel ready to retire and wondering what to do next, a small retail shop owner struggling against new competition, and a talented carpenter who couldn't get enough work after the housing market crashed. Jeff invited each person to share his or her situation and needs in just a couple of minutes and then invited brainstorming from the group for 10 to 15 minutes per person. By the end of two hours each of the six people who had come with a challenge had at least two or more solid ideas for new contacts, offers to help with a specific problem, or new directions to consider. A couple of people connected around an idea for a new business venture. Customers of the retail store gave its owner specific suggestions for improvement. The carpenter knew someone who was a great contact for the colonel, and the realtor gave the carpenter ideas for getting in on the foreclosure market. A random group of people with no obvious similarities in job interests were able to help everyone in the group in some way, and everyone came out grinning and energized.

This simple experiment reminds us of the value of investing in both close friends and broad social networks. Cross-functional teams, neighborhood groups, or random collections of those taking severance packages could well have answers for one another's problems that their closest friends and colleagues do not. As a psychologist Wendy has learned that she gets better ideas by attending conferences on the periphery of her interests than those she thinks will be most central to her work. She knows a lot about things she's really interested in, so it is harder to learn something new, whereas she gets tons of new ideas that she can apply in creative ways when she gets training from people who approach the world very differently.

Connecting us with others is one of the roles of "vital friends" at work, according to research by the Gallup Organization.[10] We all need at least some friends who play the important role of connecting us with people we don't necessarily claim as best friends. Malcolm Gladwell's "tipping points" are fueled by such people, who always seem to know somebody who knows somebody who . . . As these folks share information and bring people together, trends are born, deals are made, and ideas are cross-germinated.

Are there ample opportunities for people in your organization to come together for support and ideas and also to work independently with sufficient privacy? Are you including on your teams people whose backgrounds and ideas differ? Where do people with divergent viewpoints come together to learn from one another? Who are the connectors, and are they valued and encouraged? What problems are people facing today that others from completely different backgrounds might shed light on if brought together to brainstorm?

Resolve Conflict

When one of our kids was about seven, we overheard her in conversation with a young friend who had come to play. They were squabbling about some now-forgotten offense, and the friend threatened to "tell." Our daughter, unmoved, replied, "It won't do any good. They'll just tell us to work it out ourselves." We didn't know whether to be happy or sad about our daughter's assessment. On the one hand, we hoped it meant she understood that people, even young people, could work out their problems and that we had confidence in her ability to do so. On the other hand, we wondered if our daughter felt a little *too* alone with her relational challenges—if she thought we were unwilling to get involved and that she was on her own.

We rely on our rational thinking and empathy for others to resolve conflicts creatively and compassionately, but people vary greatly in their skill at these basic tasks. Our conflicts with one another are sparked by all kinds of differences in how we think, feel, and see the world. We have come to appreciate more and more how much people need help to learn to get along. The skills of resolving conflict and remaining cool under a perceived attack are complicated, but they can be learned.

Understanding some of the physiology of the human brain as we respond to conflict can help us have more empathy for ourselves and others in times of disagreement. First, it helps to know that special cells called *mirror neurons* help us imagine, empathize with, and mimic the emotions of others. When we feel connected with people with good emotional and relational skills, our mirror neurons help our own skills improve. Just modeling how to be cool under fire and skilled at conflict management is an asset of good leadership.

Once a conflict surfaces and we decide we are under threat (and what we find threatening varies greatly from person to person), high-power hormones like cortisol and adrenaline (epinephrine) kick in. These hormones empower the body with quick self-defensive responses—a great boon when we need extra energy or faster response time against a genuine attacker. But the same hormones, especially if chronically elevated, have a disastrous effect on learning, problem-solving skill, and empathy for others. While a certain amount of pressure or expectation increases our learning, work performance, and problem-solving ability, once we get past this optimum level of demand our performance begins to decline. Adding more pressure will not help us do better; it will only undermine our performance more.

When people have been exposed to trauma, abuse, or neglect in their early years, their brains tend to become much more sensitive to threat, abandonment, shaming, or stress, pumping out the stress hormones more readily. Such individuals then respond more self-protectively or aggressively, and they take longer to calm down after a conflict. Under the best of conditions, however, the brain circuits that promote empathy and impulse control don't always mature until the early twenties or beyond. All of these variables affect our ability to soothe ourselves when we get upset, feel empathy for others, and think objectively in the midst of conflict.

Mirror neurons are especially sensitive to the moods and perspectives of people with power, making the emotions of leaders particularly contagious at work. Leaders who are shaming, critical, or grumpy may evoke a lot of action, but not necessarily a lot of learning and real productivity. In an experiment with simulated work teams, the mood of the leader impacted not only the moods of the team members but their productivity and cooperation as well. The grumpy bosses' teams also made poorer decisions and chose less effective strategies in their panic to please the grouchy boss. Fuming and moodiness from a leader may get more work done, but it will probably not be better work. What's more, people remember negative interactions with a boss far longer and with more emotion than they remember the positive ones, so it takes a lot of positive interactions to make up for one emotional zinger. In contrast, feeling a sense of security, trust, and connection at work makes it easier to take tough feedback, solve problems creatively, take smart risks, and work through obstacles without giving up.

It is amazing how often relationships stagnate or conflicts escalate simply because people do not feel heard and understood. If you doubt this, think about an important relationship in your life. Ask yourself what the other person doesn't really "get" about you. If this person were to really listen to your thoughts and feelings on this topic, restate both the content and the feelings until you agreed that he or she had it right and had not missed anything important, would you feel more willing to really try to listen to the other person's point of view as well? Chances are good that if someone is just not listening to us, we can help the situation by really listening to him or her first.

Leaders who practice participative management recognize that participation does not always produce consensus. When two employees disagree, a leader can invite each to restate the other's point of view until mutual understanding is reached. The leader may then make a decision and move forward.

Dave learned this in working with a senior executive who had laid out an agenda for his organization in correspondence to Dave. Dave thought the executive had missed a significant point and shared this with the executive. The executive expressed appreciation for the input but trusted his own instincts. At first Dave felt ignored, but then he realized that the executive had both listened to and understood Dave's perspective. He just did not agree, and the call was his to make. Dave gave his full support to the decision. Participative management does not mean that we get our way but that we have been respected and heard. An executive once said, "I am putting you on my team because you and I do not think alike. If we both think alike, one of us is not necessary . . . and it won't be me! But when we go public, we go with one voice."

Marriage researchers wired each partner up to equipment for monitoring physiological signs of stress or relaxation and then asked them to discuss a recent disagreement. In one common pattern, one partner begins to distance from the other, showing outward signs of disinterest and withdrawal as things heat up. The other partner gets frustrated and ups the ante, raising the volume, moving closer, determined to make the distancer come back and face the music. Observers can see that the pursuer looks anxious and frustrated, and the monitors confirm that blood pressure is rising and adrenaline is pumping. But the monitors also pick up something quite unexpected about the cool, disinterested distancer. That partner's physiological signs of stress (blood pressure, adrenaline response, activation of the part of the brain that responds to a threat), though unseen, are also extreme. While the two display their stress differently on the outside, both are being flooded by intense feelings of anxiety and stress. In fact, the apparent escape artist's stress levels are so high as to interfere with clear thinking and problem-solving skill. Being chased by the outwardly upset spouse only makes the problem worse.

Some of us have seen similar patterns at work, even if the outward display of emotion is more restrained there. Only when both individuals agree to come back to the problem at a later time when their physiology has calmed down are they likely to get very far with a resolution.

Spouses, bosses, and friends can go a long way to improve the emotional climate in a given setting by avoiding what John Gottman calls the "four deadly horsemen" of criticism, contempt, defensiveness, and stonewalling. These characteristics so powerfully undercut marriages that if they show up steadily in the first three minutes of a marital conversation, researchers can predict with 96 percent accuracy that the conversation will end badly. The long-term prediction for divorce or deep dissatisfaction with the marriage follows the same pattern. In contrast, whether at work or in marriage, if conflict is managed with humor, empathy for the other person, willingness to listen nondefensively, a focus on solving the problem rather than blaming, and attention to creating an environment of emotional safety and trust, long-term satisfaction with the relationship is very likely.

As a leader, how well do you create a positive emotional atmosphere at work? (See more ideas in Chapter 6.) How well do you bring to the surface differences and conflicts inherent in any team? Are you willing to ask how people would rate you (anonymously) on how consistently and skillfully you demonstrate empathetic listening, emotional trustworthiness, appropriate humor, and encouragement of others and on how consistently and skillfully you avoid criticism, contempt, defensiveness, and stonewalling? When conflict erupts, are you a resource for helping people calm down their physiology instead of escalating their stress? Do you encourage a focus on problems and solutions instead of blame?

Make Amends

A perfect leader or a perfect friend would always demonstrate accurate and total empathy. He or she would always understand, always connect, always help. This individual would be completely trustworthy, always responding to our needs out of a deep understanding of what drives us or hurts us. Around such a person workers would always feel known, understood, and liked. Their sense of personal safety would skyrocket, along with their learning, productivity, and creativity. This is in principle only, of course. In actuality, we learn to deal with stress, problems, and conflicts in part through experience with being misunderstood, frustrated, and left—in moderate and tolerable amounts.

Unfortunately we don't live in this perfect world. Fortunately, there is a Plan B for all of us less-than-perfect mortals: apologize.

Apologizing gets a bad rap with many people, who feel ashamed, weak, or foolish when they apologize. As a result, many people have grown up with little or no experience with a sincere apology. They have yet to learn how powerful an apology can be in making up for lapses in empathy and trustworthiness. Fortunately, apologizing is a skill that can be learned, and it is almost never too late for a sincere apology to begin its healing work.

Legal departments have been nervous about admitting guilt when things go wrong for fear of lawsuits if people get the smell of blood. But current evidence suggests that doctors who apologize sincerely for even fatal mistakes are actually *less* likely to be sued, and politicians and companies are following suit. People will often see through self-serving or manipulative apologies, but many folks are deciding that apologizing is not just the economically smart thing—it is the right thing. It is still nice to know that people will not generally punish us for doing that right thing.

Of course, if apologies are not deemed sincere, they won't go far. Genuine empathy for the hurt feelings of the other person is the basis of sincerity. Once we are willing to tune in to that hurt, the steps of an effective apology are really pretty simple: (1) Say what you did wrong (if you don't know, or you don't think it was wrong, just go to the next step); (2) say what you understand the other person might be feeling and that you are genuinely sorry; (3) say what you will do to try to make it up to the person or what you will do differently the next time this type of problem comes up; and (4) ask if there is anything else you can do to make it right. After the apology, take upon yourself the onus of responsibility for helping the other person regain trust in you, especially if the problem was serious. These steps are generally effective at many levels, both personal and corporate, and generally go a long way in helping individuals, companies, even nations to let go and move on.

Abundant Relationships

There you have it: five basic skill sets that grease the skids of friendship, positive relationships, and teamwork that will promote the attendant benefits of increased engagement, productivity, and meaning. As leaders model, promote, ask about, teach about, encourage, and make room for people to care about each other, not just increased productivity, increased productivity may actually follow. High-performing teams derive from high-relating individuals.

Summary: Leadership Actions to Foster Relationships and Teams [Th]at Work
- Develop good friendships at work and encourage others to do so too.
- Learn, teach, and model the skills of
  - Making and receiving bids
  - Listening and self-disclosing
  - Navigating proximity
  - Resolving conflicts
  - Making amends
- Apply these skills to relationships between people and among teams.

CHAPTER 6

How Do I Build a Positive Work Environment? (Effective Work Culture or Setting)

LEADERSHIP **POSITIVE** **WORK ENVIRONMENT** CHALLENGE

[Organizations develop unconscious patterns of how work is done that, left unattended, may lead to cynicism, disorganization, redundancy, or lethargy. Great leaders recognize and establish positive work environments that inspire employees, meet customer expectations, and give investors confidence.]

ow long does it take to get a feel for the atmosphere in a work setting you walk into? Think of walking into a doctor's office, a store, a restaurant, a classroom, or a plant. Within minutes or at most hours you have a pretty good sense of what it feels like to work there.

Companies track employee attitudes, productivity, and retention to put numbers behind these gut impressions, but leader and customer perceptions of a work environment are often spot on. What exactly is it we are picking up on? Does it have to do with the pictures on the walls? The looks on people's faces? The casual conversations in the halls?

We've learned from personal experience (ahem!) that long-term weight loss is less about any particular diet and more about changing our lifestyle, emotional patterns, and relationship with food. Likewise, a work unit's work environment consists of the lifestyle, emotional patterns, and relationships between the people and the work that goes on there. Sometimes leaders sponsor events to try to shape how work is done (a town hall meeting, training program, annual bonus, new logo, poster and cards with vision statements, etc.), but until events become patterns, the work environment remains unchanged. The work environment reflects the organization's consciously chosen identity, brand, or culture (Chapter 3) but also shows up in the less conscious and unwritten norms, expectations, and rules—the "muscle memory" of how people think and act at work.

Most of us have personally experienced both a negative and a positive work environment. A negative work environment comes with cynicism, frustration, and gossip. Employees spend more time backbiting, protecting turf, resisting, or blindly obeying than solving problems and helping the company add real value for customers. There is an assumption of deficiency and not enough to go around of all the things that matter: resources, respect, information, opportunity. People dread work and look for excuses to be away.

In contrast a positive work environment inspires, invigorates, and challenges. Employees have positive relationships with each other (Chapter 5) and savor the work itself (Chapter 7). They see work as adding to their quality of life and personal well-being, not detracting from it. There is a feeling of abundance—enough and to spare of what matters most in our lives: good relationships, meaningful work, learning and growth, and positive impact on the world. A positive work environment is one in which:

o Employees are committed, productive, and likely to stay with the company
o Customers pick up on employee attitudes and are more likely to do business with the company
o Investors have confidence in the company's future, giving it a higher market value
o The company's reputation in the community is enhanced

In this chapter, we lay out 10 attitudes that underlie an abundant work environment and what leaders can do to foster them. Table 6.1 at the end summarizes these 10 attitudes and highlights the cynical and abundant options for each. It also enables you to score your organization on each attitude.

1. Attitude Toward Success: Arrogance Versus Humility

Recently Dave was asked to speak to a combined group of business and religious leaders. They asked his view about the dramatic economic decline that gripped the world. Not being an economist or financial markets expert, he chose to talk about the impact of leadership on this decline. When governments came to the aid of financially stressed companies with a "bailout," the metaphor badly missed the real issue. As discussed in Chapter 1, we bail out a boat taking on water or people in jail. In either case, bailouts don't solve the underlying problem of the hole in the boat or the crime committed. If the holes are not fixed or people's lives are not put in order, bailouts accomplish little.

One hole in the boat that led to recession was a lack of effective leadership. We believe one of the important qualities of effective leadership is humility. As shown in Figure 6.1, when leaders act with a sense of humility, even in the midst of success, prosperity continues. But when leaders become arrogant, prosperity reverses and declines. In many cases the success of companies and countries causes leaders to respond with arrogance, taking credit for the prosperity, seeing themselves as invincible, or focusing more on enjoying the present windfall than learning for the future. This arrogance is the pride before the fall. Humble leaders continue to improve and respond to changing conditions. And humility becomes part of the culture of the firm—the work environment we can sense when we walk in the door of a company.

There is a liability of success, and it causes many successful companies to fail. There is a rapid turnover of firms in the U.S. Fortune 500 (almost 50 percent every 10 years). Twenty years after *In Search of Excellence* was published, many of the 43 original firms had not lived up to the criteria that placed them in the "excellent" category.[1] Researchers Ulrike Malmendier and Geoffrey Tate found that CEOs who received superstar status as evidenced by public CEO awards (from *BusinessWeek*, *Financial World*, *Chief Executive*, *Forbes*, *IndustryWeek*, Morningstar.com, *Time*, Time/CNN, and the like) actually performed 15 to 20 percent worse than

FIGURE 6.1 Leadership Arrogance, Decline, Humility, and Prosperity

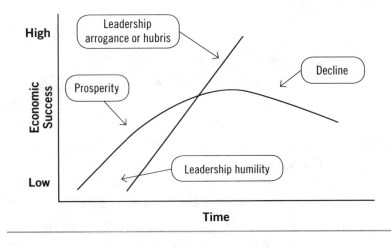

comparable CEOs for the three years after winning their award, suggesting that if such awards promote arrogance they do their recipients and their employees a real disservice.[2]

The liability of success can be overcome as leaders avoid arrogance and complacency and remain learning focused and service oriented. (See Figure 6.1.) Humble leaders take the blame for mistakes and share credit for success. They talk less about personal accomplishments and more about others' achievements. They focus on giving rather than receiving service. They don't boast about what has been but focus on the challenges yet ahead. Jim Collins in *Good to Great* notes the importance of leadership humility, labeling it a key factor in "Level 5 leadership."[3] Humble leaders have also been called *servant leaders,* who don't need to always get their way, who admit that others may be right, who express appreciation for insights, who seek to learn, and who help others do their job.[4]

Humility helps create a positive work environment of learning, service, appreciation, and growth.

2. Attitude Toward Value and Values: Implicit Versus Explicit

One of Yogi Berra's (an American athlete known for his witticisms) notorious restatements of the obvious was "If you don't know where you are going, you might wind up someplace else." Many terms have been used to articulate a direction: *strategy, mission, vision, purpose, goals, intent,* and *aspiration.* Underlying these concepts is the importance of making both value and values explicit. *Value* refers to the worth, importance, or significance placed on something by key stakeholders. *Values* are ethical norms that guide behavior. A direction statement not only positions the organization with stakeholders in the future but also suggests the beliefs and moral behaviors that will guide action to fold the future into the present. Value is about what matters to others; values is about what matters to me. A positive work environment is shaped by leaders who intentionally and thoughtfully build both value and values.

Abundant leaders must create clear and explicit value propositions for several groups: employees, customers, investors, and communities. An employee value proposition clarifies what employees give to the organization and in turn what good employees get back in return. In a positive work environment, an employee knows what is expected and what he or she can expect for meeting (or not meeting) those expectations. Negative work environments persist when employees don't know for sure what they should do or understand what happens if they reach or miss goals.

A customer value proposition clarifies what the organization intends to offer customers and what customers can expect from the product or service they purchase. Customer value propositions make explicit whether the customer should expect excellent service, high quality, technological innovation, or low prices. A high-priced restaurant will receive more complaints than a low-priced restaurant because its patrons expect better service, ambience, and food and so are more readily disappointed.

An investor value proposition states why investors can expect the company to maintain market share, remain profitable, and increase stock price. Some investor value looks back at financial results; other investor value looks forward to confidence in the ability to deliver future results. A community value proposition ensures the reputation of the organization as a contributor to the common good and a participant in civic events.

In addition to making value propositions explicit, abundant leaders have clear values statements that refer not only to ideals but also to actions. Most companies have drafted some formal statement of their values, but fewer companies have turned those value statements into leadership behaviors, organization practices, and customer expectations. In abundant organizations leaders' actions are consistent with their espoused values, turning internal values into real value for customers. A number of companies we have worked with have taken their value statements to their key customers and asked three questions:

1. **Are these the values you would like us to have?** By inviting customers to comment on the values, leaders make sure they are creating an identity consistent with

customer expectations. One company started with three key values: to be the most profitable in the industry, with great people, and great customer service. But customers didn't care if the company was the most profitable in the industry—in fact, more profit for the company meant less cash in the customer's pocket. They wanted reasonable profit so the company stayed in business but were more interested in innovative products and consistent quality.

2. **What do we have to do to live these values?** When customers help operationalize the behaviors associated with values, they become more real to everyone. Customers who operationalized *innovation* as "bold new designs" have different expectations from those who think *innovation* means "consistent improvement."

3. **If we live these values as you expect, will you buy more from us?** Values can lead to increased customer share because customers have more confidence in the firm's ability to serve them over time.

When leaders talk and act on their espoused values both inside and outside the company, employees and customers have more confidence in them. They have a sense of this being a company where there is integrity that can be trusted—enough and to spare.

3. Attitude Toward Service: Self-Interest Versus Selflessness

In the classic prisoner's dilemma game, the following scenario occurs:

Two suspects are arrested by the police. The police have insufficient evidence for a conviction and, having separated both prisoners, visit each of them to offer the same deal. If one testifies against the other and the other remains silent, the betrayer goes free and the silent accomplice receives the full 10-year sentence. If both remain silent, both prisoners are sentenced to only six months in jail for a minor charge. If each betrays the other, each receives a 5-year sentence. Each prisoner must choose to betray the other or to remain silent. Each one is assured that the other would not know about the betrayal before the end of the investigation. How should the prisoners act?

This dilemma can be summarized as:

	PRISONER B STAYS SILENT	PRISONER B BETRAYS
Prisoner A stays silent	Each serves 6 months	Prisoner A: 10 years Prisoner B: goes free
Prisoner A betrays	Prisoner A: goes free Prisoner B: 10 years	Each serves 5 years

Clearly, the best outcome for both parties is obtained if both remain silent. Each will serve six months but no more. But if one prisoner takes a chance on this option and the other does not, that individual will pay for his choice with 10 years of his life while his squeaky accomplice goes free. Acting selflessly is the best policy if everyone plays by this rule, but it is risky. If we don't trust others to act selflessly as well, we all pay a higher price. This is especially true if we play the game over and over, as companies do in real life. In that scenario people quickly learn whether trust and selflessness pay off or self-interest is the rule of the day.

133

We play many versions of the prisoner's dilemma in life . . . in divorce courts, political parties, neighborhood squabbles, and corporate mergers. Work-related examples of the prisoner's dilemma:

○ In compensation decisions about a fixed bonus pool, do leaders take a larger portion of the bonus or distribute it more widely?
○ In decision making, do leaders call the shots or include others in the process?
○ In allocating perks (parking space, travel funds, office space), do leaders send a message of self-interest or selflessness?
○ In assigning credit for successful projects, do leaders take or share credit?

When leaders consistently act out of self-interest, employees do the same. Over time, such leaders contribute to negative work environments for everyone. In contrast, leaders who emphasize other-service more than self-interest demonstrate a real commitment to treat people with fairness and respect. They help create work environments where people look out for and serve each other because people trust that the small sacrifices they make for the public good will be reciprocated, not taken advantage of. There is goodwill to spare.

4. Attitude Toward Ideas: Criticized Versus Invited

A few years ago Dave helped facilitate a town hall meeting in which employees were charged by their business leader to generate solutions to some real business challenges. After employees winnowed their ideas into recommendations, they were to present these ideas to their business leader. These employees spent most of a day generating and filtering their top priorities for sparking and supporting more innovation. When the business leader came at the end of the day to hear their recommendations, the employees were excited to share. But when the spokeswoman for the group shared the group's first recommendation, the leader slammed the table and said, "Is that all you've got to show for a day of working on this? We've tried that, and it doesn't work. I hope you have something better than that!" Needless to say, the employees' enthusiasm turned to silence and the anticipated sharing of ideas quickly evaporated. Without intervention, the work environment in this unit would sour dramatically.

Colleagues have suggested that ideas are the new economic currency.[5] The money of new ideas grows on the trees of imagination and is nurtured by encouragement, good listening, and respect, followed only later by careful, respectful pruning. Leaders who build positive work environments encourage the growth of good ideas by creating listening posts where employees share and discuss options. These listening posts may be a café-type conference area, an electronic blog, or a town hall meeting. Town hall meetings work well when leaders create a positive work environment by acknowledging employee creativity, expressing gratitude for their work, inviting open discussion of new ways to act, and making real-time decisions that demonstrate their willingness to try new things.[6]

Being open to new ideas means that leaders ask questions and seek to learn. In contrast, one leader shared his experience with a corporate executive on a two-day tour of the local facility. During the two days the local leader asked countless questions about the executive's background, experience, and suggestions for improvement. The executive, intent on sharing his wisdom and making recommendations, never asked a single reciprocating question about the local leader's perceptions or experience. At dinner on the last evening the local team shared some of its local innovations and awards from the community for its successes with plant operations. The corporate leader was surprised to learn what the local leader had done but did not pursue trying to learn about these local innovations. At the end of the trip the executive returned to headquarters satisfied that he had shared what he knew. But the local innovations were not brought into the rest of the system, and the work environment of the local team was affected more negatively than positively by the visit.

Leaders who listen and learn create an environment where ideas can be surfaced, debated, and tried. One executive is known for the yellow legal pad that he carries everywhere, to note not problems but insights from conversations in which he is always inquisitive and trying to learn. Another leader followed the flow of her product into her customer's hands, starting in her customer's purchasing department and asking why purchasing had chosen her product over others and how they could improve . . . then going to the receiving dock to determine whether her product had been shipped to the customer in ways that made it easy to work with . . . then visiting the assembly area to see how her product fit into the customer's product . . . then following up with visits to sales, marketing, and service, each time learning how her product was accessed and used by the customer. When the leader returned to her organization, she met with each group of employees to share with them the customer's comments, compliments, and suggestions about their particular area. Each group of employees felt like the leader brought fresh ideas that connected them with their customers.

A positive work environment is supported by routines that foster openness to new ideas. Employees can voice opinions and even bad news without fear of others killing the messenger. Leaders ask more questions and become a clearinghouse for innovation. Ideas are valued and sought out.

5. Attitude Toward Connections: Impersonal Versus Personal

A positive work environment is rooted in how people treat each other. In one fast-food company, local leaders had a three-step protocol for determining the friendliness of the franchise:

1. **Do our employees smile at customers?** Greeting customers, smiling at them, and making eye contact shows a commitment to friendliness.
2. **Do customers smile back?** When customers reciprocate and smile back, the friendliness is two-way and customers are probably enjoying that employee.
3. **Do customers smile at each other?** When customers engage with each other without going through the employees, they are fully enjoying the restaurant.

By analogy, employees may be seen as a leader's most important set of customers. Do leaders engage their employees in positive interactions? Do the employees engage back? Do the employees engage with one another? A positive work environment reflects all of these levels of engaged personal connection.

Ideas for creating a connected workforce are elaborated in Chapter 5. In addition, leaders build a positive work environment through caring connections by focusing on what is right more than what is wrong, expressing appreciation and gratitude, and creating ways to celebrate both people as individuals and the work unit as a whole.

Leaders can use what we call *gratitude enhancers* to help connect employees. One leader created a language that employees could use to describe their day—a simple rating scale of 1 to 10—and he would often ask, "So how is your day going, 1 to 10?" or "Did you have a 10 day today?" Another leader encouraged people to remember others' birthdays and special events. Another wrote letters complimenting employees to their spouse, children, or parents. Another started most staff meetings with a "good news moment" where people could briefly share a personal or work-related highlight. A leader who graduated from Duke University sent "blue devil" stuffed animals (the Duke mascot) to employees who had done a good job. Another leader wrote notes on personalized stationery that expressed appreciation. Another provided funds for employees to go bowling together. Another invited employees to brainstorm ways they could support a teammate with cancer. Such ideas (and many others . . . see the excellent examples by Bob Nelson[7]) help employees feel close not only to the leader but also to each other.

Obviously, leadership is not just about affirming but also about making corrections. However, we have a three-to-one rule of thumb. For every correcting comment we encourage leaders to make a bare minimum of three positive and affirming comments. This encourages everyone to focus more on what is right than on what is wrong, building a positive work environment.

The characteristics of a work environment come into high relief at times of crisis, which might include physical harm to an employee, product malfunctions, family illnesses, work-related threats, and other debilitating circumstances. At such times leaders in abundant organizations offer personal and organizational support and resources. Sanlam Investment Management is a South African investment firm. When one of its employees was tragically kidnapped and murdered, the business leader immediately reached out to her family. He also communicated to employees openly about the tragedy and offered them counseling and support. Posthumously, the deceased employee received public recognition and awards for her service, which had great meaning to her family. By recognizing and talking about the tragedy, the leader was able to help other employees pull together and cope with very difficult circumstances.[8]

6. Attitude Toward Involvement: Hands-Off Versus Hands-On

Belinda is a middle-school principal of students aged 12 to 14. A key symbol of her leadership is her tennis shoes. She spends much of her day wandering around the school. She greets students (mostly by name) when they disembark from their bus; she stands in the hallway talking to students between classes; she visits classrooms while teachers teach; she eats in the lunchroom; and she attends many after-school activities. Her tennis shoes symbolize her leadership on the run, spending time with students, teachers, and parents. Belinda's leadership priorities have resulted in lower teacher and staff turnover and higher student test scores over the course of her tenure. The atmosphere at her school has improved as teachers who are committed to education feel supported and encouraged. When Belinda's father passed away, many teachers and students attended the service to support her in turn.

While people do not appreciate a leader who micromanages, a hands-on leader can make a powerful contribution to a positive work environment. Hands-on leaders are accessible, go to employees rather than requiring employees to come to them, and get on the floor where employees are on the job. They learn what employees are doing and become more sensitive to their needs. On a recent United flight, a well-dressed passenger helped the flight attendants serve throughout the flight. Dave learned that that passenger was one of the corporate officers. Whenever he flew, he felt it was his opportunity to support the in-flight crew. Word about such efforts spreads quickly and helps employees see that they are supported.

Leaders also create positive work environments by building enthusiasm for upcoming initiatives. When Belinda greets students and teachers during the day, she often reminds them of "coming attractions" at the school. The school dances that she sponsors have high attendance because the students have been looking forward to them for many weeks. We all need things to look forward to and dream about. As leaders point people toward future opportunities, they build positive energy.

Hands-on leaders can also learn a lot about the company's work environment by becoming its customers. One company asked its leaders to call in a complaint through the normal customer service channels without identifying themselves as executives. They found gaping holes in the quality of service and preparation—holes they could set about plugging with training and supervision. The overall work environment is more positive when people know they are providing good service.

7. Attitude Toward Accountability: Enfeebling Others Versus Empowering Others

A new head of a U.S. sales operation presented his plan to the senior executive team. He was a bit embarrassed that he did not have a dramatic new program to increase sales in a tough market. What he proposed was "Management 101"—having each salesperson set clear goals for sales and make practical plans about which customers to meet with, what products to offer, and how to spend time to reach the goals. He prepared a simple one-page accountability form to use to follow up with each direct report each week. Nothing dramatic, no fancy program, not a lot of fanfare. But no one was surprised when after three months revenues began to increase. As employees began to realize that their new leader had clear, reasonable expectations and held them accountable for results, they came to trust that they could succeed.

Employees want leaders to lead, not just be peers or friends. Leading includes setting clear goals and expectations and then following up to make sure people are accountable for results. When employees participate in the expectations, they have more ownership for them. When leaders offer direct and clear feedback and help employees analyze their performance strengths and weaknesses, employees learn and move forward. When employees succeed, they have a better experience at work.

Dave was invited into a company that had gone through four new performance appraisal systems in four years, and he was asked to recommend new performance appraisal system number five. If four out of four systems do not work, it may not be the systems that are at fault but their implementation. He quickly discovered that leaders at this company were not holding people accountable for goals they set. When leaders shirk candid conversations about accountability, no system will work. We suggest three phrases that can help these conversations go better:

1. **"Help me understand."** These words put the leader in a coaching stance where the leader wants to learn, not boss. "Help me understand what went wrong" and "Help me understand what went right" both spur helpful discussions.
2. **". . . the data."** Sharing with the employee the specific data that indicate problems or successes helps everyone get results focused (e.g., missed deadlines, low customer service scores, low quality scores, low revenues).
3. **". . . so that we can solve the problem?"** gets the conversation focused on fixing the problem, not finding someone to blame. The focus is on *we*, not you or me.

When employees consistently make mistakes they don't learn from, leaders need to move decisively to replace them. When Dave interviews leaders who have been through a transformation, he asks, "If you had to do it over again, what would you do differently?" Inevitably the answer is "I would move quicker. I knew early on that X did not have the skills or commitment we needed, but I stayed with X for too long, hoping he [or she] would adapt and change."

When leaders ensure accountability, a positive work environment follows because our best experiences at work generally occur when we know we got the job done and done well. Clear accountability coupled with support for learning from mistakes helps empower people to succeed.

8. Attitude Toward Communication: Reduced Versus Increased

A common finding from employee attitude surveys is that communication rates low: employees often feel out of the loop about ideas leaders think are well understood. A positive work environment is fostered by communication that is redundant, two-way, and affectively charged.

Effective communication requires *redundancy*. When complex or new ideas are involved, it probably takes 10 units of communication for every unit of understanding. This means that leaders need to overcommunicate through multiple media. A senior leader Dave worked with crafted a detailed plan for her company. She then spent almost as much time figuring out how to share this plan as she had spent creating it: through formal webinars, teleconferences, blogs, town hall meetings, training programs, compensation programs, videos/DVDs, and staff meetings. In addition, she shared the plan informally as she talked to employees throughout her division. She invited employees to comment on the direction and to commit to the actions necessary to make it happen. At first employees were uncertain and skeptical about her agenda, but her consistent and redundant communication helped them understand the plan and see her commitment to making it work.

Two-way communication helps employees both see where the company is headed and contribute to its success. They know they have the ear of those shaping that agenda, and they are empowered to help.[9] For example, Sony regularly encourages employees to offer suggestions for improvement and seeks to implement over 90 percent of the ideas. Do workers in your company have the opportunity for this kind of impact? When employees have easy access to those who enact policies and procedures and their ideas are routinely implemented, they not only help the company succeed but know too that they are making a difference to that success.

Affect implies that information has emotional appeal. One way information becomes memorable and impactful is for leaders to share personal feelings or stories about the information. The leader described earlier who shared her plan over and over also talked about how it would affect her and others and shared her feelings about the intent and benefits of the plan. She shared stories to help employees realize that her commitment was not passive and that the plan had real consequences in people's lives.

Communication that is redundant, two-way, and affectively rich helps shape a positive work environment in which people know they matter and are motivated to contribute to the whole.

9. Attitude Toward Conflict:
Run and Hide Versus Run Into

Wendy is affectionately known in our family as "conflict averse." She hates political talk shows, resists correcting employees, and hopes that if she ignores a conflict it will go away. It is always amazing to her when people confront a conflict openly and something good actually comes of it. While it is entirely possible to create conflict unnecessarily, when we run and hide from differences, conflict often festers.

Leaders build a positive work environment by facing and running into conflict rather than avoiding and hiding from it. This does not imply escalating conflict through blame, contention, or yelling. Quite the contrary. Running into conflict rather than away from it means respectfully airing multiple points of view, being transparent about problems, and moving quickly toward problem solving when things go wrong.

Conflict may require difficult decisions. A firm saw a 30 percent drop in revenues in a recession, which led to the need for cutbacks on staff, compensation, and training opportunities. Rather than hide from this difficult conversation, leaders in this company became very transparent. They went to employee groups and shared industry conditions, customer demand, and their company's financial woes. Leaders then asked employees to help them find ways to survive the downturn. Instead of resisting and posturing, employees were highly motivated to find creative ways to reduce costs. They minimized travel, gave back vacation days, managed supplies better, and implemented dozens of other cost-cutting ideas in an effort to save jobs. When this was not enough, employees also recognized that some job cuts were necessary for the company's survival, so morale was not overly compromised.

Conflict may also occur between individuals within a work team. Leaders who sense a conflict among employees need to teach and model skills for conflict resolution. It is

145

easy to fall into shouting, blaming, and seeing only one side of an issue. Leaders manage conflict by inviting the parties into a dialogue where they seek to understand and verbalize the other's point of view until each can state the other person's position as well as the person presenting it. If clear understanding does not lead to compromise, leaders may need to make a decision, acknowledging that it may not equally please each side of the conflict. Win-win decision making requires understanding and buy-in, not agreement with all aspects of the resolution.

Setting the stage for organization-wide or individual conflict resolution means that leaders learn how to disagree without being disagreeable, accept tension without fostering contention, and allow differences while seeking common ground. When differences can be exposed and discussed, organizations have a more positive work environment because people feel safe disagreeing.

10. Attitude Toward Physical Space: Haphazard Versus Chosen

Take a quick look at your physical surroundings at work. What do they communicate about your leadership style and your company's culture? A telling example of work space sending a message is the boardroom set of the television show "The Apprentice." In each episode, contestants for a high-powered apprenticeship perform work tasks and then gather in the boardroom to meet the boss. During the boardroom showdown one of the contestants is "fired." The boardroom is dark, with no visible windows, no personal effects on the walls or table, and colors that communicate wealth and status. The board table is rectangular, with the boss and his lieutenants on one side and the aspirants on the other. The boss sits in a larger chair than anyone in the room, and he enters through a private door next to his chair so he does not have to come close to the potential apprentices. All of these visual cues signal that the boardroom is serious and the boss is in charge, surrounded by symbols of power. The use of physical space sends messages about the nature of the work environment. Here the space communicates forcefully that the boss is a man to be feared, whose word is final . . . and who needs lots of external props to reinforce his ego.

A company's work space sends an implicit message to customers and employees alike about what matters. To dissect that message more explicitly, consider layout, worker safety, lighting, color, personalization, upkeep, and symbols.

Physical *layout* can hinder or facilitate relationships, communication, efficiency, and innovation. Modular workstations let people quickly reconfigure space to meet changing requirements. What does it communicate when a company has mobile walls so that employees can organize space to form small task forces? Or when filing systems are portable to allow employees to transport materials from office to office?

Layout should include consideration of which units need to communicate or work together. If you want closer cooperation between sales and engineering, put their offices next to each other. If you want to boost creativity among your innovative spark plugs, move them near each other. The layout inside an office or plant also speaks volumes about expectations: a U-shaped table with an LCD projector in a conference room normalizes a one-way presentation to passive recipients, while a round table with flip charts and an overhead projector implies team problem solving, responsiveness, and influence based on mutual insight.

"No message" is also a message. Office layouts communicate management style and culture more clearly than any speech or culture change program. A top-floor corner office communicates a different leadership approach than a bottom-floor office near the main entrance. A leader who sits behind a desk that takes up almost half his office sends a very different message from another leader who had the desk removed entirely and works at a small table in a corner. The former meets visitors across an imposing barrier; the latter turns and interacts directly with guests.

Worker safety also plays a part in managing physical space. Investing in seating and work surfaces that fit the individual worker may be more costly than one-size-fits-all office furniture but can pay for itself in workers' compensation alone (back pain leads to almost a quarter of workers' comp claims and a third of the dollars spent[10]). A work environment that encourages employees to move around during the day rather than spend unbroken hours at their desks can make a difference in employee health. A work environment that emphasizes employee safety communicates clearly that employees are valued and their well-being is paramount.

Lighting both creates a mood and allows people to function at work. Four types of lighting may be used in the office environment:[11] (1) daylight from windows, skylights, and glass doors; (2) ambient light from ceiling- or furniture-mounted light sources; (3) task light from lamps focused on a particular area; and (4) accent or display lighting to add visual interest and define space. Natural lighting in office space helps people connect with the world outside the office and helps prevent or alleviate seasonal affective disorder, a type of depression.

Color also sends messages. Some companies pick light colors for an open feeling; others equate social status with darker colors. Red, orange, and yellow tend to stimulate and excite. Pale greens, light yellows, and off-white are calming (think doctors' offices). Water colors seem to cool things down; fire colors seem to warm the space.

People like to *personalize* their work space with favorite colors, pictures of loved ones, and mementos of hobbies or interests. Even in temporary "hotelling" offices where employees share space and furniture, some personal touches appear. Companies that ban personalization not only reduce employees' sense of ownership in their office space but risk reducing ownership in the company as a whole.

The *upkeep* of the work setting also sends a message. Is the workplace clean, freshly painted, and safe? Are the gardens kept up? Are the windows clean? These tangible details of the workplace signal commitment to quality and to employee well-being.

Symbols can also intentionally and sometimes unintentionally send powerful messages about a company. The first impression sticks: a traditional stone chalet in a forest communicates a different message from a modern glass office building downtown. The whole physical plant—architecture, location, landscaping, signage, maintenance—will be read as an indication of the company's values. Leaders with larger offices, customized wall hangings, plush carpets, rich paneling, and expensive artwork send powerful messages that fit the needs of hierarchical organizations very well. Retaining such physical accoutrements in a theoretically flat and agile organization sends the unintended message that influence is a function of position rather than a function of insight, information, and contribution.

Using these tools, leaders can thoughtfully use physical space to communicate their values nonverbally. Is the use of physical space contributing to a constraining, cold, and isolating message or to a positive, inclusive, and caring one?

Positive Work Environment in Action

Creating a positive work environment is important in all types of organizations—large and small, private and public, domestic and global. Let's look at how organizations in different settings have used the 10 attitudes (plus principles discussed in other chapters) to ensure that affirming routines replace cynical ones and that positive patterns outlive any single event.

Merck has articulated a commitment to a positive work environment with the following public statement:

A positive working environment is essential to allow our employees to achieve their potential. It helps attract new employees to Merck and motivates them to stay. Components of our working environment include numerous opportunities for employee development and professional growth, competitive compensation and benefits, our focus on health and safety, and our approach to diversity and inclusion.[12]

Their leaders then leverage the above tools to signal these values and make this aspiration a reality.

ConocoPhillips also has made a public commitment to its work environment:

> *We are committed to providing a workplace free of harassment that values employees and respects their rights. Our code of business ethics and conduct, along with our equal employment opportunity policy, set consistent global standards for providing equal opportunities and fair treatment in recruiting, compensation, professional development, and advancement. Regional policies determine how these standards are implemented in compliance with local law.[13]*

Conoco leaders make this commitment real by training supervisors to communicate openly with employees, resolve employee conflicts, and track employee attitudes. The impact of this training shows up in the work environment:

SURVEY QUESTION	% FAVORABLE	% NEUTRAL	% UNFAVORABLE
Supervisor accessible	83	12	5
Supervisor routinely discussed progress on performance goals	65	18	17
Can report an ethics violation without fear of retaliation	78	18	4

The City of Brisbane (Australia) commits to providing employees "a positive and supportive working environment," fostered by valuing diversity of people who are hired, making decisions founded on a set of values, and paying enormous attention to workplace health and safety issues. The city has publicly committed to "zero harm" to anyone in the workplace or in public places and to the health and well-being of employees through wellness programs. It offers free gyms and fitness centers in major centers. It also claims "vibrant, open office spaces that offer exciting new environments."[14]

Health care research has shown that a nurse-friendly environment leads to improved measures of not only nurse retention but also patient care. The nurse-friendly environment includes safety, control, professional development, recognition, and accountability (dimensions we highlight in this chapter). When nurses experience these "friendly" practices, patient care improves, as do indicators of nursing satisfaction, commitment, and retention.[15]

The University of Bristol's leadership team implemented a positive work environment initiative (PWE) in response to survey results from university employees. The PWE was built on five commitments to staff:

- **Staff support and development.** This includes clearly articulated standards and expectations as well as opportunities for development of employees.
- **Leadership and management.** This includes coaching leaders to engage employees and work closely with them.
- **Communication.** This includes websites and other information sharing.
- **Physical environment.** This includes paying attention to physical space.
- **Monitoring and evaluation.** This includes regular reporting of progress on PWE efforts.

As a result of these initiatives, university staff commitment scores have gone up and the university was awarded the *London Times Higher Education Leadership and Management award*.[16]

An Exercise

Walk back into your work space. Take a look around. Notice the written and verbal messages, the faces of employees, the layout of the offices, the attitudes and priorities communicated, the symbols. Take the checklist from Table 6.1 with you to help you quantify your gut impressions. Ask employees and customers to do the same. Are the messages being communicated consistent with your company's chosen values and beliefs?

Work environments matter. The work environment outlasts any individual leader in shaping how employees and customers respond to the company. Positive work environments are fostered by leaders' investment in the 10 attitudes we have described.

Summary: Leadership Actions to Create a Positive Work Environment

o   Pay attention to the work environment as patterns of how things are done.
o   Regularly monitor the work environment using the diagnostic in Table 6.1.
  •   Pick two or three of the items from your diagnosis and focus on them.
o   Ask newcomers to your work environment their impressions of what is positive and what is not.
o   Make public statements about your commitment to shaping a positive work environment.

TABLE 6.1 Summary of Cynical Versus Abundant Attitudes and Routines

ATTITUDE TOWARD . . .	DEFICIT-DRIVEN ROUTINES	TO WHAT EXTENT DO WE NORMALLY FOCUS ON	ABUNDANT ROUTINES
Success	Arrogance and taking credit	−3 −2 −1 0 +1 +2 +3	Humility and sharing credit
	Telling and demanding	−3 −2 −1 0 +1 +2 +3	Asking and learning
Value and values	Little awareness of customer needs	−3 −2 −1 0 +1 +2 +3	Clear about how we add value to others
	Core values are fuzzy or not lived	−3 −2 −1 0 +1 +2 +3	Core values explicit and put into action
Service	Taking care of self	−3 −2 −1 0 +1 +2 +3	Taking care of others
	Sacrifice is exploited	−3 −2 −1 0 +1 +2 +3	Sacrifice is rewarded
Ideas	Critical of new ideas	−3 −2 −1 0 +1 +2 +3	Open to new ideas
	Discounting employee opinions	−3 −2 −1 0 +1 +2 +3	Using employee opinions
Connections	Every person for self	−3 −2 −1 0 +1 +2 +3	Collaboration valued

		Scale	
	Friendliness is superficial	−3 −2 −1 0 +1 +2 +3	Friendliness is widespread
Involvement	Leaders are isolated	−3 −2 −1 0 +1 +2 +3	Leaders know, work with employees
	Leaders inspect or judge, don't help	−3 −2 −1 0 +1 +2 +3	Leaders are hands-on
Accountability	Expectations not clear	−3 −2 −1 0 +1 +2 +3	Expectations are clear
	Goal is to catch people doing something wrong	−3 −2 −1 0 +1 +2 +3	Goal is to catch people doing things right
Communication	Hoarding information	−3 −2 −1 0 +1 +2 +3	Sharing information
	Employees aren't heard	−3 −2 −1 0 +1 +2 +3	Employee input sought
Conflict	Conflict is ignored or escalated	−3 −2 −1 0 +1 +2 +3	Conflict is addressed respectfully
	Blame supersedes problem solving	−3 −2 −1 0 +1 +2 +3	Problem solving more important than blaming
Physical Space	Work space is neglected	−3 −2 −1 0 +1 +2 +3	Work space is functional and pleasant
	Work space is used to intimidate	−3 −2 −1 0 +1 +2 +3	Work space reflects core values

What Challenges Interest Me? (Personalized Contributions)

LEADERSHIP **PERSONALIZED CONTRIBUTIONS** CHALLENGE

[
Too often employees feel emotionally disconnected from the work they do; their work may capture their talents and time, but not their heart and soul. Great leaders personalize work conditions so that employees know how their work contributes to outcomes that matter to them.
]

hen their work is too easy, people get bored. When it is too difficult, they get anxious and give up. Somewhere in between, a moderate level of challenge and clear feedback help us stay engaged in our work, even lost in the trance of

creativity and effective problem solving. This state of flow is associated with high energy, engagement, and a sense of doing something we love, thus finding meaning that leads to abundance. Beyond the *level* of challenge, people want to work at the *type* of challenge they care about and under the *conditions* that make that challenge enjoyable. In previous chapters we discussed how identity, direction/purpose, and relationships increase the likelihood that we will find a type of work that brings us a sense of meaning. In this chapter we focus on the parameters of the work we do—the contexts and conditions that shape a specific job.

We describe in this chapter several ways of categorizing work that can help leaders home in on the type of work that works for specific employees. For example, Wendy sees herself as a healer (identity), and she finds abundance by identifying insights that help her clients change (purpose and direction). But how, where, and with whom she does her work also matter to Wendy. Does she work autonomously in a private practice or in a regulated health care system? Does she work with a narrow or broad range of clients (differentiated by age, marital status, or presenting problem)? Does she deepen expertise in a single therapeutic methodology, or does she work from a large range of counseling approaches? Does she value a consistent work schedule or want flexible hours? Such questions address the nature of her work and complement the abundance she finds from the work itself. The way she goes about doing her work has a big impact on how she feels about it.

Leaders personalize work for each employee by:

1. Understanding what outcomes matter to the employee
2. Creating a clear line of sight between what employees do and the outcomes they desire

3. Helping employees discover the intrinsic value of their work
4. Shaping work conditions and matching employees to conditions that appeal to them

Let's explore these four actions in more detail.

1. Understand What Outcomes Matter to the Employee

Often we try to motivate people by showing them how their work produces outcomes we desire without figuring out the outcomes that matter to them. Think of a parent trying to motivate a teen to clean his room, something that teenagers generally see no inherent value in and that feels to them like pretty hard work.

DAD: Your room is a mess. Better clean it up.
TEEN: I don't have time. I have a paper due.
DAD: You'll feel better if your room is clean.
TEEN: No, I won't. I like it this way.
DAD: But how can you find anything in there?
TEEN: I know where everything is.
DAD: This is ridiculous—human beings just don't live this way.
TEEN: This human being lives this way and thinks it is just fine.
DAD: Don't your friends find this disgusting?
TEEN: No. My friends' rooms all look like this.

And so the conversation goes. The parent wants the room clean, couldn't find anything in the room if he wanted to (he doesn't), thinks human beings shouldn't live this way, and knows *his* friends would find this room disgusting (and they are arriving tomorrow), so he assumes that these factors will motivate the teenager. But none of these things matter to the son. He is motivated by entirely different goals: avoid difficult work that adds no value to my life and get my paper done. Dad is trying to motivate the son to work toward outcomes that matter to Dad, but the son has other aims.

Employees are no different. The things about a job that matter to them may be entirely different from what matters to an employer or to another employee. If the leader (Dad) wants to impact the son's behavior, he needs to figure out what matters to the son and show him what behavior will lead to that outcome.

> **DAD:** Your room is a mess. Better clean it up.
> **TEEN:** I don't have time. I have a paper due.
> **DAD:** That's important. When is it due?
> **TEEN:** Tomorrow. I've been working on it, but I still have a lot to do.
> **DAD:** How can I help?
> **TEEN:** Well, could you proofread it for me when I'm done?
> **DAD:** Sure. I'll proofread if you'll work on your room. You'll need a break from writing by that point anyway. Deal?
> **TEEN:** Deal.

Other goals and interests that might motivate a teenager to clean his room: Son wants to join the Marines—Dad knows that the Marines expect a high level of personal neatness. Son wants to impress his girlfriend—Dad suspects that dirty underwear on the floor will not be a turn-on. Son wants the car—Dad can tie this privilege to room cleanliness.

Leaders who know the goals and outcomes that are important to their employees can help employees get what *they* want, not just what the leader wants. Of course employees want to be paid and to keep their jobs, but what else do they want that is impacting their behavior? Leaders can find out:

○ What problems are most pressing for this employee (or group of employees)
○ How the behavior they need from this employee might help him or her solve those problems
○ What goals or desires this employee holds
○ How the behavior they need might help him or her reach those goals

A number of years ago, Dave had an M.B.A. student who met the rigorous criteria for being accepted into a top M.B.A. program. The student often came late to class, wasn't prepared, and did not do well on papers. Dave labeled this student unmotivated, uncommitted, and unlikely to set and meet goals. Then one day he learned that this student had spent the night camping out in the cold to get early tickets to the school's football game, painted his body in school colors, and led cheers throughout the game. This individual was highly motivated and committed; it just took the right social setting to activate the "engagement gene." When Dave worked to help the student better identify with the social aspects of learning (working in teams, doing presentations, being involved in class discussions), the student became more engaged. Individuals have different ways of contributing to work. Employees may be competent (this student had high admission scores) and committed (this student chose to attend the rigorous M.B.A. program) but still need ways to contribute that work for them (this student had more passion about the social than intellectual elements of the degree).

2. Create a Clear Line of Sight Between Actions and Outcomes

When there is a clear line of sight between what we do and what we value, we find work more meaningful.[1] When living in Michigan a number of years ago, Dave and his dad decided to attend a public broadcast of a championship boxing match from Las Vegas. One of the fighters was from Michigan and a hometown favorite. The rowdy fans watching the broadcast were loudly supportive of his efforts. At about the third round, Dave leaned over to his dad and said, "I don't think he can hear us in Vegas!" All of the fans' yelling was having no impact on the outcome of this fight. This obvious conclusion dampened the enthusiasm Dave and his dad felt. Without a line of sight between their yelling in Michigan and their favored boxer's ability to perform in Vegas, their interest eroded. The hometown advantage of crowd support dissipates when the crowd cannot be heard.

In a training program, a leader did a presentation to employees on the company's stock price over the last decade. He charted stock price against earnings, competitors, capital structure, strategic initiatives, and market conditions. Participants were convinced that a higher stock price was in their best interests—they knew a higher stock price meant more money and job security for them—and they were highly motivated to make the stock price go up. But when they were asked how they could impact the stock price with their actions over the next 90 days, they were mostly stymied. Their interest and desire for higher stock prices remained high, but when they could not plainly connect their daily actions to the longer-term goal, they were like the Michigan fans at the Las Vegas boxing match: the stock exchange could not "hear" them from New York. They would look at the daily stock price, hoping that it had gone up but having little sense of influence. Not exactly a recipe for feeling that one has enough and to spare of what it takes to make a difference.

Leaders create a line of sight by crafting "if . . . then . . . " logic:

○ If my team identifies targeted customers key to our future success, then we can build better customer relationships.
○ If we create better customer relationships, we will be better able to predict and meet those customers' needs.
○ If we better meet customer needs, our revenue from those customers will increase our profitability.
○ If we are more profitable, our market share will increase.
○ If we gain market share, we will have more predictable and stable growth in earnings.
○ If we have sustainable earnings, we will gain a better reputation from investors and our stock price will increase.
○ If stock prices go up, the price of my stock options will increase, my salary will go up, or I will be more likely to keep my job.

These if/then statements help employees understand how their actions today lead to being "heard in Vegas." Employees who see how their actions today impact who wins tomorrow are motivated to keep yelling.

3. Help Employees Find the Intrinsic Value of Their Work

When leaders build a line of sight between action and outcome, employees are motivated because they want those outcomes. When work has intrinsic value, employees do the work not only because of the outcomes of the work but also because they value and enjoy the work itself. To help employees discover the work challenges they value most, regardless of outcomes, leaders can pose these questions:

o If you were guaranteed success, what work would you do?
o What do you love doing so much you'd pay to get to do it?
o What do you do that makes you feel most alive?

When the plant manager can see how her work helps her get to her desired purpose/destination of *achievement* and *impact* and enacts her identity as an arranger and maximizer, her work has value in itself apart from how many reports she completes, how much she is paid, or what hassles she confronts. Leaders who tune in to what employees want and love help them discover the intrinsic value of the work itself.

Some athletes play a game only to win; others learn to enjoy how the game is played. Athletes who play only to win may not continue to play unless success is guaranteed, but those who savor the game itself enjoy mastering techniques or team camaraderie even if no one keeps score. On the other hand, some athletes care so much about the game that they are afraid to try for fear of failing. They are highly motivated by the game, but also highly motivated to avoid the anxiety of not doing well. Great leaders help people both find what they love and manage the anxiety associated with growth and potential failure.

Work that is intrinsically motivating will generally be relatively easy, energizing, and enjoyable for that individual.

Easy

Easy does not mean without effort, but rather consistent with the employee's abilities and interests. As we mentioned earlier, Dave learned early on that his desires to be a professional basketball player were not matched by his abilities. No matter how hard he worked out, practiced shooting, or did basketball drills, he did not have the natural ability to become a professional basketball player. For him to play pro ball would be like running up a sand dune: the effort to get to the top of the hill would simply be too great. Leaders who have honest dialogues with employees about what work falls within the employee's zone of opportunity help the employee avoid sand dunes.

On the other hand, Dave had some natural talent as a teacher, and teaching came more easily to him than to others. Still, he spent (and still spends) hours observing, thinking about, and experimenting with how to better present materials when he teaches. Dave may be a "natural" at teaching, but this natural ability is supported by enormous effort. He still has to expend great effort to get to the top of his teaching game, but this is a mountain he can reasonably expect to climb.

Energizing

Intrinsically motivating work will generally be energizing. What energizes one employee may vary (insight versus accomplishment versus connection versus empowerment), but there is a high payoff for leaders who find out what gives an employee passion for the job: Is this salesman energized by making a difficult sell or raking in low-hanging fruit? Does this medical researcher care more about curing diabetes or chronic pain? Does this computer programmer get excited about really complex technical problems or really useful applications? In any work setting, individuals who find their work energizing are more engaged and more likely to be productive. Tests of work passion include the extent to which an employee wakes up excited about coming to work rather than dreading work, the extent to which an employee talks about work with a sense of possibilities rather than limitations, and the extent to which an employee gives discretionary energy to the task at hand.

Enjoyable

Intrinsically motivating work is enjoyable. *Enjoyable* does not mean liking all of the work all of the time. Every job has aspects that become routine, tiring, or draining. But big chunks of the work will be inherently satisfying. Dave likes to create words and images to make complex ideas simple and memorable. One day he was listening to a group of about 10 senior HR executives talk about their challenges. Dave noticed that many of the executives described their work using frameworks and vocabulary Dave and his colleagues had developed. He had a private moment of enjoyment in seeing his ideas have impact, even though no one attributed them to him or knew where they came from.

When leaders help channel employees into work that is easy, energizing, and enjoyable for them, their sense of abundance increases.

4. Shaping Work Conditions to Offer Abundance to Each Employee

Wendy likes one-on-one meetings with ongoing clients; Dave finds abundance in working as a presenter with large groups of strangers. Much of Wendy's work has occurred in a small office; Dave's requires extensive travel and large venues. Wendy's work requires deep connections with a few people; Dave's requires looser connections with many. Both Dave and Wendy are motivated by the purposes of *insight* and *impact*, but their preferred work parameters vary considerably. Leaders build abundance when they help each employee discover and actualize the work conditions that matter most to them. These specific work conditions vary along four parameters:

o   What type of work am I doing?
o   Where do I work?
o   How do I work?
o   When do I work?

People will answer these questions differently. A friend (Kathleen) wants to work as a toll booth operator. She imagines a job without stress that at the end of the day she can leave to pursue what really matters to her. Her skills of discipline, integrity, and comfort with routine make the toll booth her ideal job. Another friend (Leslie) graduated from a top university program. She enjoyed writing and found a seemingly ideal job at a top publishing house. But the job entailed less creative writing and more editing on a deadline. She wanted to create new ideas, not edit others' work. She was competent and hardworking, but the work did not give her much sense of meaning. She soon left. Kathleen and Leslie have very different orientations toward work and would each hate the other's ideal job. One prefers more routine and structured tasks, the other more creativity and flexibility. Each finds more abundance at work when her leaders recognize and respond to her individual preferences in four key areas—what, where, how, and when.

Work Condition 1: What Work Do I Prefer Doing?

Work can be categorized along three dimensions: intellectual, physical, and relational.

Intellectual work focuses on making knowledge productive. Knowledge workers analyze problems, discover alternatives, shape thinking, and create innovative solutions. Words and ideas become the basic elements of work that can be shaped and molded to change how people think and act. Employees who like intellectual work enjoy debates about how to shape problems and discover interesting solutions. Leslie enjoyed the pursuit of ideas, and demonstrating good use of words and insights would differentiate her as a high-performing employee in such fields. Leaders may discover their employees' predisposition to intellectual work by probing how they think about complex problems, assigning them to present verbal or written recommendations, or engaging them in a dialogue about how to assess and improve work processes. Intellectual work results in intangible outcomes that may not always be seen or measured easily.

Physical work emphasizes tangible results that are visible and traceable. Physical work emphasizes concrete, touchable results. Physical work might include figuring out what materials to use in a design, making mock-ups, and seeing products through the manufacturing and sales process. It might include on-site visits to observe how work is done. Kathleen leans toward tangible work in the toll booth, where she receives money and makes change. Employees who enjoy physical work take pride in design and production and turning ideas into actions.

Relational work emphasizes connecting with others and getting work done through others. Relational work includes helping others reflect or learn, organizing people to accomplish a task, or just bringing people together. The M.B.A. student stood out in the social setting of the football game and could bring this interest in people into his work in class. Those predisposed to relational work may like working in teams, sharing ideas with others, and creating social networks. They are connectors and brokers who engage and involve others. Leaders who recognize this social gene may help social employees become guardians of social networks and good work relationships.

While few positions are exclusively intellectual, physical, or relational, a leader may use the survey in Table 7.1 as a self-assessment to determine his or her preferred type of work or as a way to talk with employees to determine their preferred work type.

Work Condition 2: Where Do I Work?

Work occurs in many places. Traditionally, employees are "at work" when they are in the office or on the job. Sometimes employees signal their commitment by being first in or last out of the office. In a clever "Seinfeld" episode, George (the vagabond friend) had his car break down in the company parking lot. When people showed up early, his car was already there, symbolizing to them that he must be a diligent worker. When the manager left late at night,

TABLE 7.1 Assessment of Types of Work

DIMENSION	(Check One of A, B, C)					
	A		B		C	
What word describes your work preference?	Ideas		Actions		Relationships	
What work challenge would most excite you?	Drafting a proposal or report		Building a prototype or model		Being part of a team	
What work outcome would most delight you?	Someone using my ideas		Someone using my product		Someone inviting me to join him or her	
What work image appeals to you the most?	Sitting in a chair with a book		Working in a shop with tools		Engaging in conversation	
If you had a choice, how would you prefer to spend your time?	Learning about a new idea		Perfecting a new technique		Making a new friend	
Which would you prefer to work with?	Words		Tools		People	
Which would you rather do?	Plan and organize		Implement and make happen		Make others feel comfortable	
If you worked for an airplane manufacturer, which task would you rather do?	Design the plane		Build the plane		Show customers the plane	
What is the best part of your workday?	When you get time to think and reflect		When you get things done		When you share the day with someone else	
If you visited a foreign country what would you prefer to do there?	Learn about the history and culture		Participate in the local activities		Talk to and get to know the local people	
TOTAL	Intellectual		Physical		Relational	

George's car was still in the parking lot, which reinforced his hard-worker image. George told Jerry (his friend), "I don't even need to go to work! Everyone thinks I'm there because my car is!" Clearly there are more ways to be "at work" than to be parked in the employee lot. We suggest three sets of options that may (or for some employees may not) affect feelings of abundance at work: remote location versus office, inside versus outside, and domestic versus international.

Remote Location Versus Office. Some people like the formal transition from and to work, and going to an office or job site helps create boundaries between work and personal lives. But with technology, many tasks can now be done in remote locations. The boundaries of work are less about physically showing up at the office and more about delivering the desired outcomes.

A senior IBM official shared with us that at any point in time, 40 percent of IBM employees are working at customer sites, in hotels, at home, or at conferences, rather than in an IBM office. JetBlue reservationists generally work from home, where they don't have to commute or dress up to handle customer calls. Best Buy gets increased productivity and engagement when employees are free to focus on sales results, not hours in the store.[2] These strategies work well if leaders rigorously hold employees accountable for outcomes, quality, and timeliness. George cannot leave his car in the parking lot as a surrogate for commitment if the focus is on work outcomes, not hours worked. Leaders also need to consider the social elements of work, which may be neglected without face time on the job. Independent employees may become socially isolated and miss the subtle connections that make work meaningful over time.

Inside Versus Outside. The physical work environment is crucial to some people. Our contractor friend would dread work if he had to come in in a suit and tie and spend all day indoors. He thrives on working outside, moving from one project to the next, and in a casual atmosphere. We have other friends who enjoy the security and stability of their office space, perhaps using light, color, and other design elements to creatively shape the work setting.

A variant of this bias are those who travel extensively instead of working in a single location. Those who would prefer the stability of an office might find travel hassles daunting and draining; those who relish fresh challenges would find office politics demoralizing and destructive. Leaders need to help employees recognize the requirements of work and the extent to which employees and employers are able and willing to adapt to those requirements.

Domestic Versus International. Some like the comfort of a familiar culture, language, and home country. Others like the stimulation of international assignments. In a global marketplace, more people will be given opportunities to work across boundaries. Some people are energized by the challenge to adapt to new geographic contexts. Travel is a price they willingly pay to do work they enjoy. Others find travel isolating, demanding, and draining. Some homebodies can come to enjoy an international opportunity with adequate support, training, connections, and incentives.

Leaders who are aware of all these variants are less likely to impose their work style on their employees. Leaders who like to come to the office, spend time in meetings, or take global assignments will have employees who do not. When the leader adapts to the employees' preferred work setting, the chances for abundance increase. Of course, every job has certain parameters, and these are not always flexible. Periodically people tell Dave they would love his consulting job but would want to do it without all the travel. A consultant who doesn't travel is like a doctor who doesn't see patients. But the parameters of work are not always as fixed as they appear: not many doctors make house calls these days, but this used to be expected.

Work Condition 3: How Do I Work?

It is difficult if not impossible to synthesize volumes of theory and research on the nature of work into a few key principles, but let's try. We see four dimensions of how work is done that may help leaders create more abundance for their employees: innovation, autonomy, opportunity, and visibility.[3]

Innovation. Work may vary along a continuum of routine (similar work repeated over and over) to creative (doing a variety of work tasks that require innovation). Some jobs lend themselves to one extreme or the other. For example, air traffic controllers need more discipline than creativity (no one really cares if an air traffic controller can land a plane looking in a mirror between his legs). On the other hand, creative writers or product designers would not last long if unable to define and pursue blue sky opportunities. While some individuals are predisposed to and interested only in either creative or routine jobs, most are in between. Good leaders both tap employees' creative energies and help them settle in comfortably to more routine aspects of work.

173

For example, when Helen came in from the outside as a principal of a middle school, she discovered that many of the teachers had fallen into routines that were not really conducive to learning. They may have started teaching with high levels of creativity and innovation, but over time their teaching had become rote. To encourage innovation, she moved every teacher's classroom assignment over the summer. Some teachers who had been in the same classroom for many years resisted, but Helen used this symbolic change to signal new beginnings and encourage innovation. Even people on assembly lines endure the rigors of routine better if they can talk to friends, listen to music, control the pace of the line, or approach their work with humor.

Autonomy. Work may vary depending on how much control an employee has over the work done. A friend worked part time at a men's clothing store. He soon became bored with the job—who could get meaning out of selling clothes? However, the store owner was continually challenged and engaged with the work and found it stimulating and exciting. The salesperson saw his job as primarily taking orders from customers. The owner worked to figure out what clothing and styles sold the most, to create advertisements and marketing to solicit new customers, and to manage inventory to make money. The self-employed often work longer hours and have more demanding and stressful jobs than their employees, but they find more meaning in their work because they have control. Employees can sometimes feel the same sense of ownership if they participate in an aspect of the work that they can control and benefit from, if they see the complete job versus one element of it, or if they have a say in key elements of their work experience.

At the other extreme, one executive team (which will remain unnamed) told us they as executives had vast experience within their industry that enabled them to solve problems better than anyone else in their firm. They isolated themselves to define what should be done and how to do it and then shared their wisdom with their employees. Describing this highly centralized governance process, an executive quipped, "We sort of believe in 'designed by genius, implemented by idiots.'" It is not a shock that their organization had higher employee turnover, lower morale, and less productivity than competitors.

When employees participate in defining and solving problems, they are more committed to their decisions. We refer to shared decision making as the fingerprint test. A leader wants a lot of employee fingerprints on a project or initiative so that employees are a part of the governance process and multiple perspectives and types of expertise are included in solutions.

Opportunity. Work varies according to how much the employee can grow from the work. While some employees prefer steady jobs with little change, most want the chance for growth and challenge. The more common opportunity choice is the extent to which an employee wants to either broaden or deepen skills. Some employees would like to become deep specialists who have extensive expertise in a particular area. Other employees like the chance to learn a little about many types of work. To determine how employees define opportunity, Beverly Kaye suggests leaders have a "stay" interview with employees where they ask, "What would it take to keep you both on the job and passionate about the job?"[4]

A senior manager asked his financial head this question and discovered that she wanted the chance to run a business. When reassigned as a business leader, she flourished. She not only grew the business beyond expectations but also experienced personal growth in her new role. Employees have opportunities for growth through temporary job changes, project assignments, professional development experiences, promotions, or other challenges at work. Leaders give employees opportunities for growth by asking employees to do difficult things that might be outside their comfort zone. Then leaders need to give employees transparent and honest feedback on what worked and what did not. While outwardly inconsistent with the "build on your strengths" mantra, this approach assumes that employees who do new things may build new strengths.

Visibility. Work may vary according to how much visibility or recognition the employee gains from doing the work, both inside and outside the company. In Philosophy 101 we ask, "If a tree falls in the forest and no one hears it, did it make a sound?" In Abundance 101, leaders ask, "If an employee did a good job and no one noticed, did it contribute to the employee's sense of abundance?" Sometimes employees are so self-motivated that they only want to prove to themselves what they can do. But more often employees want to be recognized for their contributions. If the Olympics were held in private, Michael Phelps might still have won 14 gold medals, but his impact on the world of sports and its impact on him would have been reduced.

Leaders need to recognize good employee performance appropriately and publicly. Some of this visibility shows up in reward systems as bonuses and promotions, but the visibility also comes from immediate feedback and public praise for doing something well. Small comments and sincere expressions of thanks can make a difference. When a participant in an executive program in China complimented Dave on his course, Dave joked that the participant should tell Dave's mother. Dave was surprised and pleased when a week later his mom told him she had received a call from someone in China who had been in his course and wanted to thank her for her son's work. Visibility, recognition, praise, and positive feedback allow leaders to communicate gratitude to employees for their work.

Just as soldiers in the heat of battle think more about saving their friend than saving their country, workers who feel valued and appreciated by those they work with are more engaged even if their jobs seem relatively detached from their broadest values. When leaders structure positions, match people to positions, design management processes, and communicate broadly about innovation, autonomy, opportunity, and visibility, employees can tune in to ways that their work matters to both the world at large and to the individuals they work with.

Work Condition 4: When Do I Work?

Dave and Wendy each have pioneer ancestors who crossed oceans and continents to colonize a new land. In today's work world, pioneer boundaries are less about space and more about time. Time has often become people's scarcest resource and most valued asset, and many companies today are pioneers in its use. How we spend our time communicates our values and priorities.

Calendar Test. When Dave coaches senior leaders, he often asks them to do a time audit or "calendar test":

- In the past 30, 60, or 90 days, what would you say were your top priorities?
  - What did you talk about in your public speeches?
  - What were your stated goals?
- What percentage of your time did you spend on these issues?
  - Whom did you meet with, and what were the topics of conversation?
  - What were the agenda items in your meetings?
  - What else did you spend time on, and how important were those things?

This calendar test helps leaders know if their intentions are consistent with their actions. A leader once said that his priorities were building stronger customer relationships, but his calendar made clear that he spent most of his time inside his organization in meetings and planning sessions. Another leader claimed managing cost was the priority, but this priority did not show up in her calendar.

Hypocrisy is a leadership killer. Employees pay more attention to behavior than rhetoric and will observe what leaders do more than what they say. Leaders build abundance by living up to the values that give meaning to work, including the value of integrity between their intentions and their calendars.

A new leader wanted to send a message to his organization about the importance of inclusion in the workplace. Instead of just talking about the value of inclusion and diversity, he regularly scheduled meetings with employees in underrepresented groups, asked for data on the careers of these employees, and sponsored projects that communicated inclusion. Wendy often ends a session by asking the client how he or she might spend fifteen minutes to make progress on goals. Even busy people can find 15 minutes, and without at least some commitment to action more talking only fosters the illusion of change without the reality. Dave likes to end his workshops with a cartoon of a group of turkeys who have just attended a training seminar where they learned to fly. They spent time flying and soaring among the clouds. Then, the caption says, "at the end of the seminar, they all walked home." Dave often asks workshop participants to share the action items they have calendared and to schedule a phone call or e-mail follow-up with a peer to ensure accountability for the result.

Satisficing. Herbert Simon, a Nobel Prize–winning economist, used the term *satisficing* to describe decision making based on meeting the minimal criteria rather than on searching for an optimal solution.[5] Leaders should also help employees invest their time, not just spend it. We have used a simple formula, "return on time invested," as a time quality check. In one company, when leaders make a request of employees, the employees are encouraged to ask "how much time is this request worth?" By answering this question, the leader can signal the amount of time and the rigor of the decision the request warrants. Sometimes leaders make innocuous requests that create volumes of work among employees because leaders are not clear about the return on time invested and what should be satisficed versus optimized.

Most of us have learned to satisfice (versus optimize) some personal decisions. We might satisfice making our bed or taking care of our yard while optimizing our relationship with our children. We might satisfice on breakfast and optimize on dinner. Leaders can help employees know when to satisfice and when to optimize by having the "return on time invested" discussion. Some organization initiatives and decisions are so important to do that they are worth doing well (e.g., safety in manufacturing, customer relationships), but other still-important decisions don't require as much precision.

Flexibility. One key to managing time is schedule flexibility. Many employees want flexibility so they can respond to demands from their personal life. This does not mean that they will work fewer hours, but it may mean that they can have some say in when they work those hours. As employees make choices on work flexibility, they are constrained by business realities (not many in a grocery store want to work on Friday or Saturday nights, but someone must). But employees are often very motivated to find creative ways to get work done well if they can have some say about when to do it. Many organizations have options for four 10-hour days or even three 13-hour days to allow employees to build a work-week that works for them.

Abundant Work

A relative of ours has a fridge magnet that states: *Life's greatest tragedies occur when we give up what we want most for what we want now.* Sometimes what we want now is so basic to survival that putting off what we want most is a noble sacrifice and not a tragedy at all. But generally speaking, our work feels most abundant when we get both some of what we want now and much of what we want most. Even in good times no one has a perfect job, and even great jobs have unpleasant aspects. In a down economy the type of work we can get and the parameters of that work may be even more constrained, leaving employees feeling that they are giving up more and more.

In good times or bad, great leaders can help employees find a line of sight between the work they do and the outcomes that matter to them. They can help them find the intrinsic value in doing work that matches their skills and interests. They can help shape the work space and the duty roster to increase options, control, and flexibility for employees. They can help employees connect with the aspects of the work that come most naturally and that are energizing and enjoyable. The assessment tool in Table 7.2 offers a template for doing this diagnosis and matching.

An abundance-seeking employee can also use this assessment tool to think through what conditions of work matter most and what conditions can be satisficed—finding a reasonable option rather than a perfect one. He or she will also recognize that production requirements dictate many aspects of work, making compromise necessary. An employee can create a personal work scorecard based on this assessment that informs work choices.

As leaders and employees work together to match tasks and people, there will always be gaps and snags—aspects of the work that are unpleasant, unclear, or uninteresting to almost everyone. As employees participate in these discussions, they can often find creative solutions for sharing such tasks or changing their parameters. When leaders don't take this initiative, they risk losing good employees over

TABLE 7.2 Work Characteristics Assessment

Assessment: What Work Challenges Me

QUESTIONS ABOUT THE CONDITIONS OF WORK	FEATURES: TO WHAT EXTENT DOES MY WORK . . .	TO WHAT EXTENT DOES THE EMPLOYEE WANT THIS FEATURE? LO 1 2 3 4 5 HI	CHECK THE THREE WORK CONDITIONS MOST CRITICAL TO YOU	TO WHAT EXTENT DOES THE JOB REQUIRE THIS FEATURE? LO 1 2 3 4 5 HI
What work am I doing?	Offer me *intellectual* challenges?			
	Offer me *physical* challenges?			
	Offer me *social* challenges?			
Where do I work?	Allow me to choose to work *remotely* (on the road or at home)?			
	Allow me to choose to work *in the office?*			
	Allow me to choose to work *indoors?*			
	Allow me to choose to work *outdoors?*			
	Allow me to choose to work *domestically?*			
	Allow me to choose to work *internationally?*			

How do I work?	Allow me to be *innovative?*			
	Allow me *autonomy?*			
	Allow me *opportunity to grow?*			
	Allow me *visibility?*			
When do I work?	Enable me to pass the *calendar test* (match my priorities to how I spend my time)?			
	Enable me to know what to *optimize versus satisfice?*			
	Give me *flexibility* in my work schedule?			

sometimes trivial aspects of work that are more flexible than they realize or that people would feel better about doing once they knew they had been heard and their suggestions considered. Of course a leader should be clear about what must be done to deliver results, compete in the marketplace, and fairly distribute rewards. But engaging employees in shaping their work where possible empowers them to get some of what they want now and much of what they want most. This is abundance at work.

Summary: Leadership Actions to Ensure Personalized Contributions to Work

- Learn what outcomes matter to employees: How does this job relate to their identity, values, and purpose?
- Help employees articulate the line of sight between what they do and the outcomes they value.
- Help employees discover the intrinsic value of their work and what they enjoy in the work itself.
- Shape work conditions and match employees to conditions that appeal to them (where, when, with whom, and how they work).

How Do I Respond to Disposability and Change? (Growth, Learning, and Resilience)

LEADERSHIP **GROWTH, LEARNING, AND RESILIENCE** CHALLENGE

[As changes compound and the risk of failure increases, people may fade, fail to adapt, and get demoralized, which leads to organization stagnation. Great leaders relish change and help employees grow, learn, and be resilient to bring new life to their organizations.]

hange happens.

Consider the following from Tim Clark's research detailed in his book *Epic Change: How to Lead Change in the Global Age.*[1]

- The cost of a gigabyte of computer memory dropped from $10 million in 1956 to $7,700 in 1990 to $13.30 in 2000 to $1 in 2006.
- Sales of white bread in the United States fell slightly from $2.3 billion in 2001 to $2 billion in 2005. In the same time period tortilla sales rose from $81 million to $1 billion—a 12-fold increase.
- One in eight couples married in the United States during 2005 met online.
- In 1976, Americans drank an average of 1.6 gallons of bottled water per year; in 2006, the average was 28.3 gallons.
- More than half of the Ph.D.s awarded in the United States in science and engineering go to students from China, India, Korea, and Taiwan.
- Ed Lawler also found that between 1973 and 1983, 35 percent of the top 20 companies in the Fortune 500 were new; 45 percent were new between 1983 and 1993; 60 percent were new between 1993 and 2003; and if the last five-year trend holds, over 70 percent of the top 20 Fortune 500 companies will be new to that list for 2003 through 2013.[2]

All of these changes and the millions more they represent take us into new territory, where the likelihood of failure increases. Deficit responses to change are rooted in fear, stagnation, and withdrawal, born of the belief that failure is a threat to success. Abundant responses to change focus on learning and resilience, born of the belief that failure is a path to success.

A classic example of this second mind-set is Thomas Watson, Jr., who headed IBM in the 1960s. A manager reporting to Watson ran a business unit that lost $10 million.

Watson called him into headquarters. The guy walked into Watson's office weak-kneed. Watson said, "Do you know why I called you here?" He responded, "I assume you called me here to fire me." Watson said, "Fire you? Hell, I just spent $10 million educating you. I just want to be sure you learned the right lessons."[3]

Another story is told of Jonas Salk, the inventor of the polio vaccine. When asked where he got the resilience to persevere through multiple scientific failures, he referred to his mother. He remembered a time as a child when he was eating cookies and milk while zooming a toy car around the table. His mother warned him repeatedly to move his milk away from the edge of the table so he wouldn't spill it, but he ignored her. Predictably, he knocked the milk to the floor. He looked up, chagrined. Most parents would have scolded a child for ignoring warnings. Salk remembers his mother simply asking, "So, what did you learn?" The importance of learning from failures stuck.

These stories exemplify an abundant response to failure. Rather than use change and setbacks as an excuse to scold, punish, give up, or give in, leaders who build abundance focus on learning and resilience.

No one becomes a better musician, teacher, scientist, carpenter, dentist, accountant, or manager without stretching outside of their comfort zone. The only way to avoid the setbacks and disappointments inherent in this unfamiliar territory is to avoid trying new things. Frankly, if you are not failing at something, you are probably not pushing yourself hard enough. What's more, failure should be disappointing. If there is no disappointment, the work you tried was probably not that important to you. We have coached leaders to "rejoice in disappointment" because disappointment means they are working on things that matter to them.

Our self-esteem and capacity to cope have more elasticity, or capacity to stretch without breaking in response to stress, when we have a learning mind-set. Just as a savings account gives us elasticity in the face of unexpected expenses, Stephen R. Covey refers to an "emotional bank account" that gives us elasticity in the face of unexpected setbacks of other kinds. When people learn how to learn from mistakes, they can cope better with the stress of change. Setbacks become opportunities to grow rather than reasons to give up. Leaders build this elasticity, this sense of having enough stretch and to spare in one's emotional bank account when they teach employees how to learn from both good and bad experiences. A learning focus puts *new meaning* on failure and change in general, turning it from a threat to an opportunity. This learning focus, rich with meaning making, is a key building block of the abundant organization.

Learning

Think of someone you would characterize as a gifted learner. Why? What are this individual's personal attributes? What can this person do?

Rand is one of our most precocious learning friends, as he exemplified when traveling with us to a foreign country. First, he was constantly inquisitive, engaging the local residents to find out more about their lifestyles and beliefs. Second, he wanted to try new things: on our one-week trip he learned the alphabet of the local language and began to learn the basics of the language so that he could communicate better with the people. Finally, he could use insights from one setting to understand another: he enjoyed contemplating how the experiences of the Maccabees in the first and second centuries B.C. apply to today's political environment. Rand demonstrates not only high intelligence but learning agility—the ability to inquire, experiment, and extrapolate in flexible and productive ways.

Organizations need learning agility as well—an organizational capability for making knowledge productive. Organizations with high learning agility are not only more interesting places to work but also more profitable. Dave has defined *organizational learning agility* as the ability to generate × generalize ideas with impact. At either a personal level (our friend Rand) or an organizational level, these two principles help people build a learning response to change:

o **Generate.** Leaders who encourage learning seek new ways to do new things. In the face of change, they are open to experimenting, adapting, and improving.
o **Generalize.** Leaders who learn transfer ideas from one area to another. They have the ability to see patterns that may apply elsewhere.

In a world of increasing change, a learning focus both increases employees' elasticity for responding to setbacks and opens up new opportunities for growth and contribution.

Principle 1: Generate New Ideas

As change occurs in the business environment, yesterday's rules of thumb become outdated. When leaders encourage

189

the generation of new ideas and procedures, they build learning agility. We have identified four ways leaders generate new ideas: self-reflection, experimentation, continuous improvement, and boundary spanning.

Self-Reflection

Learning leaders are self-aware. They recognize that their choices have consequences, and they constantly review both the choices they make and the consequences of those choices. They ask themselves questions such as:

○ What can I learn about myself from what just took place (in a meeting, conversation, or presentation)?
○ What did I do in this setting (meeting, conversation, work effort) that worked? Why?
○ What did I do that did not work? Why not?
○ Is this how I generally respond to similar situations? What are my common patterns?
○ What could I try instead? What am I afraid might happen if I change?
○ If I am sometimes successful at a different approach, how could I be more consistent?

By asking these types of questions, leaders enhance their learning agility. They also model for employees how to be inquisitive, open to suggestions, and committed to improving.

Self-reflection shows up as well in leaders' willingness to be accountable. When they make mistakes, learning leaders run into them rather than away from them. They also help others reflect on their goals and take responsibility for reaching them. When goals are missed, learning, not blaming, becomes the priority.

Experimentation

Leaders encourage experimentation and innovation by asking employees for their input and encouraging employees to try out their ideas. Employees with successful track records get more latitude in experiments. Experiments are bounded in time and space and audited rigorously to determine how well they work. Experiments may occur in a number of areas: product design and features (e.g., Microsoft Office), service (e.g., FedEx), channel of distribution (e.g., online purchases), operations (e.g., Walmart's supply chain), cost management (e.g., lean manufacturing at Herman Miller), customer experiences (e.g., Starbucks), management processes (e.g., virtual teams at Nokia), business model (e.g., direct distribution at Dell), or industry redefinition (e.g., iPod at Apple). Experiments that don't work should be abandoned, with lessons learned transferred to other settings and without lingering investments in the unsuccessful experiment.

Learning leaders also accept difficult and new assignments where they ask lots of questions and are resourceful and creative in approaching traditional problems. They are open to alternatives rather than locked into habits. These leaders generally have many interests both inside and outside of work.

Google employees work aggressively on building a culture of experimentation or innovation. They have identified 10 attitudes for innovation that capture their commitment to experimentation:[4]

1. Ideas can come from anybody.
2. Share everything you can (new ideas and projects are put on the Internet).

3. Dare to recruit somebody more powerful and insightful than you.
4. Have a green light to your dreams: commit one day a week to contribute to the company the way you like (50 percent of new initiatives are developed during this day).
5. Look for quick wins.
6. Provide less "I like it" and more analytics.
7. Do not kill an idea; transform it.
8. Innovation requires constraints like budgets and timelines.
9. Care about the end customer first, not the money.
10. Identify your "twin" in the company . . . an innovation sparring partner.

With these attitudes and actions, Google has a remarkable track record of experimentation and innovation.

Based on work in the innovation literature, we have identified a six-step protocol for experimentation. (See Figure 8.1.) Leaders who use these steps help employees discover that there is always enough and to spare of great ideas.

Continuous Improvement

Continuous improvement programs are just what they sound like: efforts to institutionalize the focus on constant improvement. Leaders encourage continuous improvement through both formal programs and informal conversations.

A great example of a formal continuous improvement program is Alcoa's suggestion system where thousands of suggestions are made and about 60 percent are implemented. Over 40 years, Toyota's suggestion system has received more than 20 million suggestions or about one per employee per week, the vast majority of which are used. The GE Work-

Out initiative and town hall meetings were designed as a disciplined way for employees to share ideas for removing unnecessary work and improving work processes. While no system is flawless and mistakes and recalls may hap-

FIGURE 8.1 An Experimentation Protocol

Step 1: Idea Generation

Experimentation originates with fresh, out-of-the-box streams of ongoing ideas. Leaders inspire new ideas by:

○ **Focusing on the needs of potential users of ideas (customers).** For example, innovations in health-care delivery may come as leaders experience receiving health care as patients.

○ **Encouraging risk takers.** Ideas also come from the iconoclasts in your organization—individuals who are passionate about experimenting with new approaches. Make space for them.

○ **Forming alliances.** Ideas come from loose associations that span departments and bring people of different perspectives and training together.

Step 2: Impact

Experimentation is more than new ideas; it is about ideas with *impact*, so rigorously filter ideas using the following criteria:

○ **Strategic fit:** Is this idea consistent with our business plan and identity?

○ **Potential value:** Will the financial return potential justify further resources?

○ **Opportunity size:** Will the value and impact be large enough to make a difference?

○ **Service:** Will the innovation help us provide better service?

○ **Employee passion:** Will our employees have the passion and competence to pull it off?

Step 3: Incubate

Ideas that pass the impact screen merit additional care and feeding. Learning leaders create "incubators," where the idea can be piloted for acceptance and technical feasibility. Failures are almost as important as successes, since they prevent investment in ideas that look promising only on paper. To foster experimentation, one firm put in place the mantra "Think big, test small, fail fast, and learn always." The leader found that the firm did worst on "failing fast" as many ideas that would not work endured beyond their useful life span.

continued

FIGURE 8.1 An Experimentation Protocol *(continued)*

Step 4: Invest

Successfully piloted ideas are ready for further investment. An expanded field test is one way to ensure sustained value before gearing up for a full product or service launch. Strategic investment will require clarity around services, distribution channels, and geographic scope.

Step 5: Integrate

For experimentation to endure, new ideas need to be integrated into old. With product innovation, this means that new products and/or services both complement and cannibalize the old, and both must be dealt with realistically. With strategic innovation, it means that new business models become commonplace throughout an enterprise. With administrative innovations, practices that worked in one division must become integrated across an enterprise.

Step 6: Improve

Experimentation does not end but evolves. It requires successive improvement where lessons learned are constantly codified, adapted, and implemented. Leaders committed to learning constantly monitor the product life cycle. Is the experimentation still creating value? Quarterly or semiannual reviews of product, strategic, or administrative experiments can focus attention on the next wave.

pen, these approaches enable employees to feel personal ownership and accountability for business results.

Leaders can also sponsor continuous improvement informally through what they attend to and ask about. One of the most useful questions leaders can ask when an employee poses a problem or question to them is "What do you think?" Generally (not always), the employee has spent more time thinking about the problem and potential solutions than the leader. When leaders give employees license to solve the problems they identify, employees find more meaning in their work.

Boundary Spanning

Leaders can look for best practices both inside and outside their organization. It is not enough to share a best practice, however; we must also consider the system in which the practice works. For example, many copied GE's town hall meeting initiatives, only to find that they were not as successful unless accompanied by many of the other GE management practices (incentives, succession planning, leadership training, teamwork, etc.). Also, copying someone else's best practice automatically means trailing in generating new ideas. Even better is to leapfrog a best practice, improving it before implementing it to move beyond what others have done.

Steve Kerr introduced us to a learning matrix methodology to determine best practices inside a company that can be shared across geographic, functional, or business boundaries. (See Figure 8.2.) This matrix uses five steps:

1. **Complete this statement: To be world class at X, we must . . .** X can be anything the corporation is committed to doing well (e.g., service, quality, customer focus, cycle time, or training). This steps identifies 10 to 12 factors critical to success in X. A small research team, task force, or other group can define these 10 to 12 critical success factors, which become the columns at the top of the matrix.

2. **What are the units where these factors could be demonstrated?** These units are organizational entities (functions, plants, divisions, geographical areas, etc.) where the critical success factors could be demonstrated. These units become the rows listed on the left side.

195

FIGURE 8.2 Learning Matrix

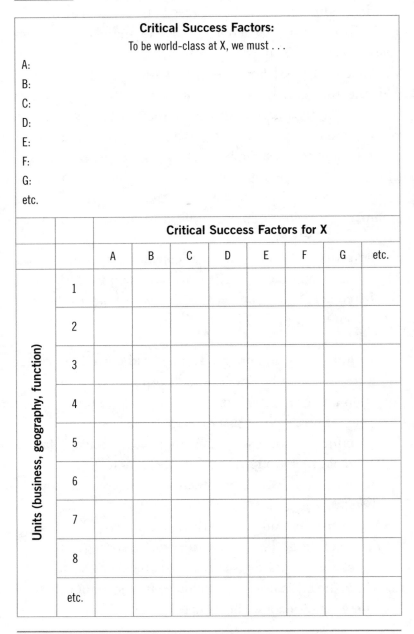

3. **For each cell, rate that business unit on that critical success factor as follows:**

> 0 = not applicable
> 1 = not good at all
> 2 = below average
> 3 = average
> 4 = we think we are good (self-report)
> 5 = others think we are good (certified by someone else as excellent or world class)

This assessment can be done either by an organizational unit leader or by an external rating team (e.g., a corporate group that inspects the unit or an outside rating agency). Scores of 0–4 can be provided by members of the organization unit; a score of 5 must come from outside.

4. **Combine the individual assessments by rows or columns.** The ratings for each cell may now be combined to create a learning matrix for a particular initiative (X). The average score for a row indicates how the particular business unit fares. The average score for a column indicates how well the entire organization is doing on that particular factor. This matrix helps pinpoint pockets of excellence as well as an overall corporate score for a particular initiative. It can be used to track progress on initiative X across business units or across factors.

5. **Create processes for sharing ideas from high scorers with lower scorers.** Mechanisms for sharing knowledge and experience across cells include:
   o Make the higher-scoring business units "best practice" sites where others can learn.

197

○ Create cases from the higher-scoring cells for others to draw on.

○ Move talent from higher- to lower-scoring business units.

○ Create incentive systems for sharing knowledge (e.g., bonuses, awards).

○ Assign someone from corporate to oversee the entire matrix process and ensure that a larger percent of cells are 5s in each successive year.

This learning matrix offers a disciplined way to share best practices within an organization.

When leaders use a mix of self-awareness, experimentation, continuous improvement, and boundary spanning, they help their organizations learn from rather than be overwhelmed by change.

Principle 2: Generalize Ideas

Generalization simply means the movement of ideas or knowledge across boundaries like space or time. For example, our friend Rand readily transfers his skill at learning languages into new geographic settings and brings his understanding of ancient civilizations into today's political processes.

Most of us are not nearly this good at generalizing knowledge or skills. The biggest challenge in education is not to get kids to learn math but to get them to remember to apply the math skills they have learned when they go to the grocery store or restaurant. Research on continuing education programs suggests that most participants, even though they spend a lot of time and money and even if they rave about the program, will change very little as a result of their investment and enthusiasm. Helping employees (and ourselves) generalize learning by applying it in new settings and spreading it around is not easy. But without this key step, generating great ideas is a waste of time.

In organizations, leaders move knowledge across many boundaries: vertical (from the top to the bottom of an organization), horizontal (from one function, department, or business to another), external (from supplier or customer), global (from one geographic site to another), or temporal (from one time period to another).[5] Leaders generalize learning across these boundaries by buying and building talent, creating incentives, and using information systems.

Talent

Organizations are only as gifted at generalizing ideas as the individuals who compose them. Robert Eichinger and Michael Lombardo have identified 68 competencies of talented employees. These competencies are based on a content analysis of dozens of studies and competence models. Specific competencies of individuals who help organizations generalize ideas across boundaries include:[6]

12. conflict management
27. informing
32. learning on the fly
33. listening
36. motivating others
46. perspective
48. political savvy
51. problem solving

Firms can either *buy* or *build* these generalizing competencies. To *buy* these generalizing competencies firms can hire outside talent either full time (as employees) or part time (as contracted consulting or outsourced partnerships). A *build* strategy for competencies involves training or developing existing employees. A build strategy assumes that with appropriate nurturing, current employees can acquire competency at sharing knowledge. Moving talent across units is a common build practice for sharing knowledge, such as through a succession planning system that lets employees apply for jobs or projects throughout an organization. Using training events as forums for sharing ideas and turning them into action also facilitates generalization. Some innovative companies today are not only moving people across units within their company but also doing executive exchanges between their company and customers or suppliers. Procter & Gamble high-potential leaders who need more savvy in technology may exchange roles for two to six months with Hewlett-Packard executives who want to improve on brand management. These and other ideas are listed in Table 8.1.

Incentives

The old adage "People do what they are rewarded for" is half helpful. Without doubt, incentives change behavior. But incentives work to accomplish business goals only when they are based on clear and explicit standards. A better adage would be "Incentives promote business goals when people are rewarded according to clear and measurable standards relative to those goals."[7]

When incentives link rewards to clear standards for learning agility, learning agility will increase. Start by measuring

TABLE 8.1 Checklist for Acquiring Talent for Learning

BUY *To buy learning and generalization skill, we . . .*	BUILD *To train for learning and generalization, we . . .*
☐ Hire outside experts as consultants	☐ Attend as teams rather than individuals
☐ Acquire new competencies by hiring skilled full-time employees	☐ Focus on learning application not just knowledge acquisition
☐ Hire and promote curious chiefs	☐ Attend in cross-functional groups
☐ Seek fresh blood (from universities, competitors, oddball places)	☐ Invest in ongoing education throughout the organization
☐ Follow the whims of superstars (but insist that the stars share)	☐ Involve customers in all aspects of training
☐ Formally recognize learning (e.g., "Director of Knowledge Management")	☐ Share ownership of training between line managers and HR
☐ Hire people known as learners with competencies such as inquiry, reflection, systems thinking, mental modeling, conflict management, disciplined postmortem processing, ability to make data-based recommendations, networking	☐ Plan training to stretch participants intellectually and practically
	☐ Use training forums to challenge work assumptions and processes
	☐ Require systems training for all employees
☐ Outplace nonlearners and tell people about it	To continually develop employees, we . . .
☐ Promote learners in the hierarchy and give them public recognition	☐ Use postmortem format to learn from experience: What did you learn? What will you do differently as a result?
☐ Leave people in jobs long enough to demonstrate learning	☐ Sanction cross-functional moves
☐ Source candidates for every position from multiple sources	☐ Support learning sabbaticals
☐ Put people with varying backgrounds into management positions	☐ Rotate people across jobs
	☐ Encourage innovative job assignments (e.g., start-up, turnaround)
	☐ Participate in task forces
	☐ Practice external job sharing (share employee with customer or supplier)
	☐ Assign people to special projects
	☐ Have on-the-job apprenticeships
	☐ Ensure that every person has a learning plan

learning agility (perhaps using relevant criteria from this chapter); then build this measurement into the performance management system. Once standards and measures are established, allocate rewards for meeting those standards. Some rewards are financial (e.g., base pay increases, bonuses, stock options), and others are nonfinancial (e.g., recognition awards to managers who anticipate competency needs or demonstrate learning strategies). As long as rewards tie to the measures of learning agility, accountability for learning increases. A good example of an integrated system for innovation and learning agility is 3M's "vitality index," which measures the percentage of revenue that comes from products introduced in the last five years. This vitality index encourages experimentation, risk taking, and sharing of ideas. In this light, measures and rewards may also be used to encourage cross-boundary behavior. One company requires that 20 percent of the bonus money available to a leader to distribute must be given to someone outside his direct chain of command. This money pool allows leaders to rewards boundaryless behavior.

Information Systems

Many large professional service firms have created the position of "Director of Knowledge Management," whose primary responsibility is to move information across units. Accenture (a consulting firm) excels at leveraging technology best practices across business sites. On completing an assignment, each Accenture consultant answers basic questions about the assignment:

○ What was the presenting problem?
○ What methods were used to deal with the problem?

○ What were the results?
○ What were the lessons learned?

These answers are merged into an ever-evolving data set that other consultants may draw on. Accenture's consultants live and work all over the world, but they still form a community of values because they share so much information. The Accenture database they draw on becomes a carrier of the values of the firm.

The two principles we have laid out—generate and generalize—help leaders build elasticity in employees by increasing learning agility. With a broader range of skills, employees can better cope with change. They come to see change as offering opportunities for growth more than excuses for failure. When employees learn, they have enough and to spare of the information, confidence, and skills not only to perform but also to contribute at work.

Resilience

Resilience is the ability and courage to bounce back and try again when faced with change. One of the greatest examples of resilience is U.S. president Abraham Lincoln. Born into poverty, Lincoln faced defeat throughout his life. He lost eight elections, failed at two businesses, and suffered a nervous breakdown. Here is a sketch of Lincoln's road to the White House:

> 1816: His parents were forced out of their home. He had to work to support them.
> 1818: His mother died.

203

1831: He failed in business.

1832: He ran for the state legislature and was defeated.

1832: He lost his job. He wanted to go to law school but couldn't get in.

1833: He borrowed money from a friend to begin a business and lost it all by the end of the year. He spent the next 17 years paying off his debt.

1834: He ran for the state legislature again and won.

1835: He was engaged to be married when his fiancé died and his heart was broken.

1836: He had a total nervous breakdown and was in bed for six months.

1838: He sought to become speaker of the state legislature and was defeated.

1840: He sought to become elector and was defeated.

1843: He ran for Congress and was defeated.

1846: He ran for Congress again and won. He went to Washington and did well.

1848: He ran for reelection to Congress and was defeated.

1849: He sought the job of land officer in his home state and was rejected.

1854: He ran for Senate of the United States and was defeated.

1856: He sought the vice presidential nomination at his party's national convention and got fewer than 100 votes.

1858: He ran for the U.S. Senate again and was defeated.

1860: He ran for, and was elected, *president of the United States.*

Clearly, Lincoln not only learned from setbacks but demonstrated almost inconceivable resilience. His biographers have described the emotional strengths that contributed to his enormous resilience:

○ **Empathy:** He could put himself in the place of others and appreciate their point of view.

- ○ **Humor:** He used self-deprecating humor and storytelling to put people at ease.
- ○ **Magnanimity:** He held no grudges against those who disagreed with him.
- ○ **Generosity of spirit:** He publicly admitted mistakes and took blame for administrative errors.
- ○ **Perspective:** He put things in context, always seeing the big picture.
- ○ **Self-control:** He controlled his public emotions, sometimes by writing a letter to himself and then tearing it up.
- ○ **Balance:** He was able to relax and entertain friends even in the midst of stress.
- ○ **Social conscience:** He tirelessly worked to serve others.[8]

Lincoln's resilience enabled him to cope with huge setbacks and try again, somehow maintaining the perspective that he had enough and to spare of what it would take to succeed.

Consider three sources of resilience that leaders manage to create meaning from loss or failure: personal, social, and organizational.

Personal Resilience

Leaders facing the same challenge may respond with despair or resilience. Personal resilience, the ability to bounce back from defeat, increases when leaders can do the following:

- ○ **Maintain an optimistic attitude.** Resilient leaders see opportunity even in the midst of dramatic change. Lincoln used humor and stories to communicate optimism in the face of the enormous challenges facing the

Union. For an immediate boost to your sense of well-being, try this exercise that will likely have demonstrable results: Each night for a week, write down three good things that happened that day and why you think they happened. Stopping to notice things we like about the day, especially when we also notice what caused the good moment, is a great routine that builds hope and connection.

○ **Live out of a strong moral code.** Many of the most resilient victims of hurricane Katrina and 9/11 attributed their response to their faith and moral compass. In times of distress leaders can turn to lasting moral principles to get their bearings and rally others. Lincoln appealed to moral values in his memorable speeches, placing present action steps in that context:

> With malice toward none, with charity for all, with firmness in the right, as God gives us to see the right, let us strive on to finish the work we are in; to bind up the nation's wounds; to care for him who shall have borne the battle, and for his widow and his orphan—to do all which may achieve and cherish a just and lasting peace among ourselves and with all nations.

○ **Face fears head-on.** We have a friend who gets very anxious in social settings. Rather than run from the fear, she invites people to her home. She has done the same with her fear of needles by training to be a phlebotomist; of exercise by committing to do a triathlon; and of performing by auditioning for community theater. Leaders who face anxiety or other fears or challenges directly increase their resilience and skill.

- ○ **See patterns and put events in context.** When the Union lost a battle, Lincoln continued to focus on winning the war. He knew the long-term outcome that he desired and could accept periodic setbacks as long as he moved forward. Leaders see beyond single events into longer term patterns.
- ○ **Stop worrying and start living (quoting Dale Carnegie).** To gain resilience in the face of change we have learned to ask ourselves, "What is the worst thing that can happen?" Once we identify and stare down the worst-case scenario, we can better move forward.[9] When leaders accept the possibility of the worst and then act to create the best, they move forward with more resolve.
- ○ **Manage risk.** One of the liabilities of transparency is that leaders' private actions become fodder for public discussion. Transparency demands may reduce the willingness to take risks, and bold actions that create innovation may be tabled. Resilience is, almost by definition, willingness to take risks. Our formula for risk taking is *will to win divided by fear of failure.* Will to win often comes from personal predispositions and the ambition or drive that an employee might have. Leaders can ensure a high will to win by selecting and placing the right people in the right jobs, but they may take more directive actions to reduce the fear of failure. Rather than punishing mistakes, leaders need to help people learn from them. The Tom Watson story at IBM is one of many examples of leaders who reduce the risks of failure by focusing on learning rather than blaming.
- ○ **Move on.** Sometimes resilience comes through managing the transitions associated with change. William

207

Bridges points out that a transition is more than a change of behavior; it is a change of identity and patterns. Real transitions require emotional processes, not just behavioral modifications. These emotional processes include:

- Letting go of old identities, activities, assumptions, and relationships; mourning the loss of the "old normal" that will not be regained
- Putting up with a sometimes lengthy period of confusion, uncertainty, and redefinition of roles; gradually coming to imagine and experiment with new patterns, identities, and ways of making decisions
- Allowing something new to be born, institutionalized, and valued as a "new normal" rather than clinging to the past

Symbolic acts can help facilitate this difficult transition process. Belinda, the school principal, changed teachers' classrooms as a symbol of a "new world order" at school. Another new leader facing a major corporate transition asked employees to list on a card the things they had done to contribute to the company's past success. He encouraged employees to share these stories with friends and family for a weekend. On Monday morning he invited everyone to write him a personal memo on what he or she would do to help implement the new agenda. Then they all burned the cards representing the past. Leaders who take seriously their meaning-creating role of honoring the past and boldly envisioning the future help others complete the transitions related to change.

Social Resilience

A few years ago, one of Dave's books was reviewed on Amazon. Here is the verbatim review:

> **Stupid title. Stupid theory. Stupid book.**, *September 15, 2003*
> *Reviewer:* **PT Kearns** *from UK*
> *We all need to worry when "top" academics are telling us that the bottom line isn't. At last, the vacuity of Dave Ulrich's work is plain for all to see. Any book which states that the "big, new idea is connecting leadership to market value" (p.259) has to win the award for the most fatuous statement of the blindingly obvious.*
> *I was going to give this 0 stars, but the system does not allow it.*

Ouch. When Dave read this review, he was mortified, angry, and hurt. His first reaction was to cover the computer screen with his hand so no one would see it. But of course the review was already in the public domain, hanging out there for all to see. So instead of pretending to hide the review, he started to share it. He learned that most people did not agree with this reviewer (thank goodness), and he got social support to cope with the negative comments.

Another time, Dave received a prestigious award. A later write-up of the ceremony began, "Dave Ulrich, a large and homely man . . ." Again, he shared the unflattering description with his wife and friends, who jokingly said that he might someday change one of these two factors (large), but he was stuck with the other (homely). Sharing difficult situations lets close friends laugh with us and give us perspective—or perhaps help us change. When Dave decided to become "less large," he publicly shared his commitment to a large group of young adult missionaries he was supervising at the time. He held up an Oh Henry! candy bar and said, "I am working to lose weight and not eat any more of these great candy bars. If you catch me eating an Oh Henry! bar, you can drive my car for a day." Over the next few weeks, Oh Henry! bars appeared in his briefcase, car seat, pockets, office, and nightstand with the names of those making the offers attached. But, with his public commitment (and car insurance premiums) on the line, he was able to resist.

We all need social support to be resilient in managing change. As we have discussed in previous chapters, there are two types of social support: close and loose. Close friends support us and remind us that we are cared for even if we are "large and homely." What a privilege to have friends who don't care as much about what we do as about who we are. Leaders and employees who surround themselves with close friends get support for change. But, in addition, we need loose connections with more distant acquaintances who teach us new things. After 35 years of marriage, Dave and Wendy can order for each other at restaurants and often fill in the blanks of open-ended sentences. We need new associates who offer new ideas on how to approach old problems. We can find new connections through professional associations, extended social groups, and new assignments. By having close friends who support them and new acquaintances who teach them, leaders can find social support to manage change.

A final way to build social support for change is to help someone else manage change. When we help others, we often become more able to cope. We build a goodwill account with others that we can later draw on. We see the change through someone else's eyes and get a different perspective. During a crisis, those who join groups to help others gain support themselves. Mothers Against Drunk Driving (MADD) is indispensable to many who have lost a loved one in a car accident. By serving others, they become more resilient.[10] Those who formed similar groups after 9/11 coped better with the painful transitions of that crisis.[11] Leaders can ask those struggling with a transition to help others through it. By serving others and giving back, those experiencing difficulty may cope better.

Organizational Resilience

Leaders who build organization systems that reinforce resilience and increase capacity for change practice three principles.

Principle 1: Make the Unspeakable Speakable. Anyone in a long-term relationship has discovered that without candid conversation the relationship withers. To build a relationship, caring partners need to talk. This is especially true for things they don't want to talk about—things that make them embarrassed, resentful, or doubtful. But only when we make the unspeakable speakable do real understanding and empathy occur.

In almost every organization "unspeakability" viruses limit successful change. These unwritten and unspoken norms dictate activity and prescribe choices without full awareness or choice. Dave and his colleagues have identified more than 30 such viruses, including these:

○ **Activity mania.** Our badge of honor is a full calendar, even if it excludes thinking and results; we hide behind our busyness.

211

- ○ **Have it my way.** We insist things be done as we want, not allowing other styles.
- ○ **False positives.** We hide behind nice-talk, even when we disagree.
- ○ **Authority ambiguity.** We are not sure who is responsible or accountable, so no one is.
- ○ **Turfism.** People defend their turf, sometimes to the detriment of the overall organization.
- ○ **Full sponge.** We are overflowing with too many changes going on at once; we are burned out and stressed out on change.
- ○ **Overmeasure.** We measure everything, even to a fault; our dashboards are way too complex.
- ○ **Undermeasure.** We don't have indicators to track important stuff; we measure what is easy, not what is right.
- ○ **Going for the big win.** We look for the mega-change that will solve all problems instead of starting small with low-hanging fruit to build momentum.

When leaders can identify, name, and discuss such viruses openly, they can be cured. New employees often see these viruses most readily, just as we see the clutter in someone else's home more readily than in our own. Teams can have fun naming, drawing, and mocking viruses lurking in their organization. One team drew their most prevalent viruses, then posted these drawings in their offices while they worked to disable them.

Principle 2: Turn What We Know into What We Do. In managing change in organizations, most leaders can accurately list within two minutes 7 to 10 keys to successful change. In our work, we have synthesized a number of keys to successful change, including the following:

- **Leadership.** Change requires a strong leader who sponsors and champions the change.
- **Felt need.** When the need for change is palpable, it helps overcome the natural resistance to change.
- **Vision.** A clear and compelling vision based on clear values and with specific goals and action steps facilitates change.
- **Commitment.** Get people to act as if they are committed, and commitment will follow.
- **Decisions.** Build a decision protocol that breaks the vision of tomorrow into decisions today; start with small, visible changes to let success build success.
- **Systems.** Institutionalize a change through wise investments in people, communication, rewards, information and data, and budget.
- **Measures.** Monitor how the change is going to ensure learning and adaptation.

Knowing what it takes to make change happen does not mean we will do it, however. Leaders help people turn what they know into what they do by bringing the discipline of a change checklist to any project and initiative. Pilots, surgeons, merger specialists, and fast-food restaurant managers all use checklists to ensure consistent performance. Leaders can use a change checklist to determine what keys to successful change are already in place or where to invest more resources. For example, in one company, the first three keys to change from the preceding list (leader, need, and vision) scored high, but decision protocols, systems, and measures scored low. This team did not need to spend more time on selling the change but did need to invest in how to make it happen. In another case, leaders scored high on all the change disciplines, but employees did not. In both cases, change checklists helped leaders ensure that knowledge about change was turned into action.

Principle 3: Make Change a Pattern, Not an Event. Ultimately, organizational resilience and learning in response to change is not about a single incident but about creating a new pattern. Learning cannot be something that just happens in a workshop, team meeting, or process review; it must become part of the soul of the organization, something that occurs naturally and continuously during all work activities. A pattern implies that a new culture has been created, a new vision institutionalized.

Corporate cultures that abound with resilience and learning inside generally focus on customers outside. Customers' needs, values, options, and dreams always take us to the cutting edge of innovation and improvement. When this customer focus is embedded throughout the organization, learning and resilience become systemic. Change is not an idle hazing meant to distract employees, but an essential link to keeping up with customer expectations and delivering value in the marketplace.

In Conclusion

Change happens.

How we respond to change matters. (See Table 8.2.)

TABLE 8.2 Change Assessment

Am I a Change-Able Leader?		
PRINCIPLE	**DIAGNOSTIC**	**SCORE** LO 1 2 3 4 5 HI
Learning		
Generate ideas	How much do I experiment with new ways to do things?	
	How well do I continuously work to improve?	
	How often do I seek out new ideas from others?	
	How self-reflective am I?	
Generalize ideas	How well do I transfer ideas from one setting to another?	
	How well do I institutionalize practices for sharing ideas?	
Resilience		
Personal	How readily do I bounce back from setbacks?	
	How consistently do I show an optimistic attitude?	
	How well do I act from a strong moral code?	
	How often do I see patterns and put events into context?	
	How well do I work at an appropriate level of risk?	
	How well do I know when it is time to move on?	
Social	How transparent am I about the challenges of change?	
	How comfortably do I share my challenges with friends?	

continued

215

TABLE 8.2 Change Assessment *(continued)*

		SCORE					
PRINCIPLE	**DIAGNOSTIC**	LO	1	2	3	4	5 HI
Social	How much do I tap broad networks of loose connections?						
	How well do I help others with their change challenges?						
Organizational	How readily do we turn what we know into what we do?						
	How well do we implement systems for learning from failure?						
	How well do we make change into a pattern, not an event?						
Total							

An executive recently said that a business that took 50 years to build could be lost in 2 if it does not respond to change. Individuals, teams, and organizations that respond to change with learning and resilience have a chance to succeed; those that do not may lose the ability to catch up. As leaders institutionalize the ability to generate and generalize ideas with impact, organizations become resilient at individual, social, and organization levels. Patterns of learning and resilience equip organizations to respond to external demands, create higher intangible market value, implement strategies, and plan for the future. They also create excitement and a sense of abundance among employees by infusing them with a sense that this organization has enough and to spare of the intellectual, social, emotional, and organizational resources to meet real needs and make a difference for good.

Summary: Leadership Actions to Facilitate Growth, Learning, and Resilience

○ Have a positive attitude about change; trust that you can learn from it and be resilient when facing it.
○ Learn how to generalize new ideas through:
  ● Self-reflection
  ● Experimenting
  ● Boundary spanning
  ● Continuous improvement
○ Learn how to generalize, or share, new ideas by:
  ● Moving talent across boundaries
  ● Sharing information across boundaries
  ● Building incentives to encourage shared behavior
○ Become resilient in the face of change by:
  ● Making the unspeakable speakable
  ● Turning what you know into what you do
  ● Changing events into patterns

CHAPTER 9

What Delights Me?
(Civility and Happiness)

LEADERSHIP **DELIGHT** CHALLENGE

Partisanship sometimes affects organizations where there is more hostility than civility and where a we-they, win-lose, right-wrong, blame-and-shame mentality persists. Great leaders move away from hostility and intolerance toward multiculturalism through problem solving, listening, curiosity, diversity, and compassion and by bringing creativity, pleasure, humor, and delight into their organizations.

Recently, Dave's father, Richard Ulrich, passed away. As the family gathered to celebrate his life, we were joined by an interesting assortment of individuals whose work was far removed from anything Richard did professionally: bank tellers, produce managers, teachers, and folks who worked the window at McDonald's. Why? Because when Richard went to the grocery store for peaches, he did not just see someone putting out produce. Richard saw an individual with a name, a story, and a personality. He saw someone he could get to know, make smile, sing a song to. His favorite song was "You are my sunshine, my only sunshine, you make me happy when skies are gray . . . ," and he sang it off key but with gusto. By the end of his life he walked only with the help of braces and a cane, yet he regularly gathered day-old baked goods from local grocery stores, as he had done for over 20 years, loaded them into his old truck, and delivered them to shelters and soup kitchens all over town. He never missed his grandkids' games. He picked up stranded strangers and gave them a lift. He brought flowers to his wife every week (until she pointed out to him that she was allergic to them). Of the hundreds of people at his funeral, virtually every one had received a personal letter from Richard, usually written at 3:00 A.M., thanking them for some small service or offering some tidbit of counsel or encouragement. In his honor, we gave everyone who came to the funeral a McDonald's coupon to give away to someone who needed a hamburger or an ice cream cone. Kind of a silly thing to give away at a funeral, but Richard loved to give such things away. Richard was a character, but he knew how to find delight in the world and loved sharing it with others.

So what does giving out McDonald's coupons or singing to the bank teller have to do with how leaders build your company's bottom line? Just this: Customers who are delighted with their interaction with our products come back for more. So do employees. In an understated, backdoor way, delight seems to go to the heart of finding a sense of abundance at work. Delight teaches us that life's goodness is not found in money or fame but in simple pleasures, meaningful connections, and a sense of discovery. Delight reminds us that no one has nothing to give, that relishing diversity and multiculturalism is good business, and that there is always something of which we have enough and to spare. Employees who find delight at work are often employees who stick around, who make a difference, and who invest their discretionary energy in the creative and challenging aspects of work.

When we talk to leaders about the ideas in this book, the idea of making room for delight sticks. It smacks of creativity, playfulness, pleasure, and fun. It is approachable, reachable: "I'm going to bake cookies and take them to work tomorrow—that'll shock people!" "I'm going to learn more people's names, and not just the people above me on the organizational chart." "I'm getting a book on tape for the commute home and turning off the talk radio." "I want to thank someone sincerely every day." "I am going to have a dress down day at the office." "I am going to begin staff meetings with a good news, non-work-related moment." These simple choices remind them that harder choices can also be broken down into more manageable pieces, that they are not alone, that they have a capacity for creativity and change that doesn't emerge only when strong-armed by relentless production schedules or hefty rewards.

Delight is not just about jokes or cookies, although it is about jokes and cookies. Delight is about noticing little things, breaking out of ruts, feeding creativity. Delight is about appreciation, about beauty, about playfulness and fun. Delight is picking up the cell phone to check in—or maybe turning off the cell phone to check out. Delight is doing someone a favor, choosing a new screensaver for our computer, taking day-old bread to a battered-women's shelter, picking berries with the kids. Delight is about appreciating and learning from people who come from different backgrounds and cultures. Delight may start with a leader's sense of humor or from a group of employees who find joy at work.

And delight can turn a tough day on a tough job into something tolerable, something laced with hope. While delight is inherently personal, we can manage a common process to figure out what it is. Leaders can do this exercise alone or with their employees. Take out a pencil and a piece of paper. Ready?

Number from 1 to 10. As quickly as you can, list 10 random changes you could make to bring more delight into your life. And if you find yourself resisting this suggestion, let us warn you that there are more of these exercises to come in this chapter, so, hey, humor us. It will take only two minutes, and it might be delightful. Go.

Did you do it? If not, why not? Need some suggestions to get started? Here's Wendy's list: take a walk after dinner, offer to babysit our grandbaby once a week, write a novel, walk through the backyard, take a yoga class, go to the farmers' market, get a new pen, call my sister more, trace my genealogy, drive up the canyon with good music on.

Here's Dave's list: spend time weekly with each of our children and our granddaughter, walk up the canyon, offer tips ($10 or $20) to good flight attendants, take a bike ride, read a novel, attend more Jazz (basketball) games, check in daily with Mom, Google an interesting topic just to learn about it, exercise regularly, give talks on new subjects, take time off to stroll along a beach.

Maybe some of the things you wrote down require a hefty amount of disposable income, but we're guessing that much of what brings you delight is about small and simple things, not big and expensive things. In fact, research on what makes people happy backs up that idea. If they were to get a windfall of $20,000, most people think they would get the biggest kick out of shooting the wad on a big vacation or plastic surgery or front-row tickets to a play-off game. And it is true that the big purchase would get your attention and give you a huge thrill and a lasting memory. But the research suggests that after two years you would have gotten a lot more satisfaction and a bigger boost to your overall happiness by investing $100 a week in lots of smaller hits: small vacation breaks, dinners with friends, gifts for people you like, handouts to someone in need, a membership at a gym, fresh flowers, a new basketball, a painting class—especially if you keep the small hits consistent with your values and interests.

So, how many of the items on your list were related to or done at your work? Too often, delight is found outside of the daily demands of work. In a workshop, senior leaders were asked to write their personal leadership point of view. In almost every case, when leaders talked about values and things that brought meaning and delight to them, they referred to things outside of work—their children, families, hobbies, and service activities. When they talked about work, they referred to their ability to set goals and get things done. Simply stated, we want to bring meaning and delight into work, without minimizing the seriousness or intensity of the work we must do.

Delight at work does not have to be expensive either, and employees will generally appreciate lots of small investments in their well-being and delight at work more than grand gestures on rare occasions. As a leader you set a tone for cultivating and modeling delight at work. You can also ask others to brainstorm about what they could do to make work more fun for them or what the company could do at minimal cost that would be meaningful to employees to bring delight to work.

Let's look at four sources of delight that can make work, and life, more enjoyable: creativity, pleasure, humor/

playfulness, and civility. Then we'll talk about how fostering delight at work among employees can also create a climate of delight for customers.

Creativity

Delight is both an outcome of and a contributor to creativity. This is a chapter about finding delight, not using delight to build creativity, but the process certainly can go both ways. If we know we want to foster creativity at work, then providing people with rich images and evocative raw materials will invite the creative part of them to come out and play. We do our best sustained creative work under moderate, not severe stress, when the heat is on but we are not in the pot. As long as the challenges of staying in business and keeping a job are sufficiently motivating, an atmosphere of playfulness, humor, and support can keep things from boiling over.

But creativity is also delightful! When we have a creative breakthrough, a moment of innovation or novelty, we often get a huge charge out of it. It sparks delight to see a solution that has evaded us, to realize a connection we hadn't made before, to be surprised by truth. If we want to find work delightful, even small doses of creativity enrich the stew.

In many organizations creativity is the domain of research and development. It is not really fostered on the plant floor or in the accounting office, where in fact creativity is suspect. Who needs a creative accountant? You do. Even if you don't think accounting creativity will help your bottom line, it can help your employees, who can help your bottom line. Like this:

Creativity experts Julia Cameron and Mark Bryan describe Jerry, an accountant for a Big Six accounting firm. Jerry reports, "My life was lackluster. I knew it but lacked the will and resources to change it. I crunched numbers by day, in a place that felt like a tomb, and I ate cookies at night to calm my fears of being dead." Jerry took a course in creativity from Julia and Mark and was assigned to spend time each week feeding his creative interests. He couldn't think of any. He did other assignments, but he was not experiencing the usual jump in delight that came as people invest in their creative lives.

Then Jerry remembered a long-forgotten curiosity about Oriental rugs. He began to explore rug stores on his day off. He was fascinated. The romance and timelessness of caravans moving across the deserts sparked his imagination. Being the good accountant he was, he began to study the rugs, learn the rules about what made them valuable, and run the numbers on rugs he liked. One day he found a rug in a secondhand store that he quickly realized was a steal. He bought it, took it to work, and put it in his office. He writes, "That first rug transformed my office and my life. It gave me something to talk about with clients, and I suddenly understood in a visceral way what my job really was. I was supposed to help clients turn their money into beauty, things they dreamed of. I suddenly had new respect for my job and new respect from my clients. I learned to listen to the beauty in the numbers. . . . I help clients manifest their dreams."[1]

Creative accountants not only help find creative answers to problems that bore most of us; they bring a sense of meaning and delight to colleagues and customers. Creativity on the plant floor may mean the difference between turnover and retention, between business as usual and innovation, between line-stopping problems and back-saving solutions. People shouldn't have to work for Disney to have the chance to be imaginative, innovative, or inspiring at work.

Creativity with a capital C may be the domain of artists, scientists, and high-paid marketing firms, but garden-variety creativity is what lets everyday people know and *feel* we are alive. It is what helps us figure out what to do when our kids won't do their homework or our employees won't finish their paperwork, without alienating either. It is what opens doors to new relationships and new endeavors. It is not just about doing something we have never done, like eating a grasshopper or swearing at the president. Creativity is about bringing divergent ideas together to solve a problem, articulate truth, capture beauty, or form a promising connection that leads to new products and better ways of doing business. And that sparks a sense of delight in everyone who touches it.

Creativity expert Eric Maisel writes:

> [Creativity] can have its own splendid rewards, but the goal is to produce work that has meaning and makes meaning in the universe, that touches and transforms others, that speaks to others, that decorates or enriches the lives of others, that bears witness—that, to put it in the most old-fashioned way possible, is both beautiful and true . . . each of us knows that the special marriage of truth and beauty, where witness is borne and material crafted, is the very definition of deep work and high achievement.[2]

Both playfulness and civility can be seedbeds for creativity. Playfulness invites irreverent questions and fresh approaches that spark new ideas, while civility moderates the tone of harshness or criticism that can keep innovation from growing. To be sure, not every brainchild is worth developing, but even the best ideas do not see the light of day without encouragement and protection. Creativity requires curiosity and reflection. It requires working outside your comfort zone and attempting things where you may not be qualified today. It requires hard work and deep honesty. Most of all, it requires us to learn to tolerate anxiety. Eric Maisel states:

> *While anxiety is the greatest impediment to aliveness, in order to create you must invite anxieties into your life and live anxiously. . . . If you are to create you must invite anxiety in. But then you must manage it.*[3]

Do you remember anyone in school or your early job training teaching you about the anxiety that accompanies honest, creative work? Do you remember anyone telling you how to manage that anxiety, tame it, work despite it? Most of us don't. This is often the great leader's job: to help people tame and tolerate the anxiety inherent in the process of doing good work, creative work, meaningful work. Leaders can warn people about difficulties, stir up hope in the face of obstacles, and hold open the space between a vision and its realization to help people trust that it can happen. Great leaders not only help shape that vision or identify those problems but also help people muster the stamina and courage to keep trying, to keep staring down their self-doubts or fear or boredom until they get somewhere new.

Questions for you:

○ **Who are your most creative employees?** What do they need to work creatively? (More clarity about what is needed or its parameters? More help? More experience? More license? More encouragement? More protection from criticism in the early stages? More realism?)

o **Who are your least creative employees?** What do they need to work more creatively? (Consider the same possibilities.)

o **Which category do you fall into?** What do you need to work more creatively?

Pleasure

Positive psychology guru Martin Seligman has identified three sources of happiness: things we find deeply meaningful, things that are deeply engaging, and things that simply feel good. While lasting happiness is not found in pleasure alone, in balance with meaning and engagement pleasure contributes a lot to our sense of well-being, including at work.

Number your sheet of paper from 1 to 10 again. What are 10 things you could do to make work more pleasurable that would cost nothing or less than $20? Ignore all judgments about whether these ideas are practical or even possible— just brainstorm and see what comes up. Go!

If you are having trouble getting started, try deliberately including at least one item from each of the following categories of pleasure: physical, intellectual, spiritual, social, and emotional/aesthetic.

Here are some of the things we've heard:

o **Physical.** Play air Ping-Pong with Fred in the hallway on breaks, take a walk at lunch, burn scented candles in the lobby, keep a golf ball and a putter behind the door, stash chocolate, organize a yoga class, rearrange my office furniture, do sit-ups.

○ **Intellectual.** Ask people about their favorite books, get a new iPhone application, learn new vocabulary words, set up a friendly debate, study a language, look more stuff up on the Internet, Google myself or a friend, attend a conference or class in a field I don't know much about, read more, listen to people I disagree with until I can clearly articulate their position.

○ **Spiritual.** Organize volunteers for Habitat for Humanity, privately pray for coworkers, pool money with office-mates to support a disadvantaged child, play Gregorian chants in the elevator, fast for world peace, give fast-food coupons to homeless people, post and practice the values our team believes in, plant trees, get out the vote.

○ **Social.** Invite some new employees to a picnic lunch, start a sudoku contest, tip a good flight attendant, go bowling as a work team, become a better listener, compliment people more, do an act of unsolicited service for someone you care about, make a real connection with someone every day, respond more to others' bids, share ideas more.

○ **Emotional/Aesthetic.** Smile more, take good pictures and share them, plant flowers, find a great screensaver, get colored file folders, bring in a headset and some good music, get an office pet, sponsor a company talent show, write in your journal and share it with your family or friends, have a poetry contest, make more jokes, tell patriotic stories.

Will any of these things save the economy or improve your market share? Not immediately. Could bringing pleasure to work get out of hand? Of course. But somewhere in between saving the world and disintegrating into an overgrown frat house, pleasure has a role to play in making work a place where people feel good about being alive and being at work. Leaders set an important tone in encouraging, modeling, participating in, and sometimes toning down or rechanneling pleasure and delight at work so they serve a greater good.

○ Do you know what the primary sources of pleasure at work are in the preceding categories for each person on your team?
○ Do you know which departments have the most turnover? What are the sources of pleasure at work that matter most to those who leave? To those who stay?

Humor and Playfulness

Everybody had a favorite teacher at school. Occasionally these were people who were intellectual giants or deeply caring mentors, but often our favorite teacher was the one who was funny. Humor and a sense of playfulness can make the serious work of business more palatable for everyone. John Kotter at the Harvard Business School is a world expert on change. He has written a number of important volumes on the process of change, books that get quoted in academic articles and look impressive on bookshelves but don't sell a lot of copies. Then Kotter decided to write a lighthearted parable about penguins who realize their iceberg is melting and something will have to be done. Embedding his message about the steps of corporate change in an approachable and playful little story would not work very well if Kotter didn't have something worthwhile to say, but adding humor and accessibility to his considerable academic credibility allowed Kotter to significantly broaden the impact of his ideas. *Our Iceberg Is Melting* has sold more than 500,000 copies.

Of course, if your work setting already struggles to get people to put down the whoopee cushions and get down to business, you will have to take this section with a grain of salt (or maybe consider how to channel that lighthearted-ness into friendly competition or great customer relations). If your office needs to present a high degree of decorum to convey an appropriate professionalism to clients, playfulness may have to be reserved for the commute home (or maybe ask yourself whether all clients really want *all* that propriety *all* the time). To start, put an X to indicate where you would currently put your company or team in terms of playfulness, humor, and fun:

Frat house wannabe   **1 2 3 4 5 6 7**   Funeral home on Valium

Now, where do you think your best customers would like you to be? Circle that number. Finally, what would your best employees prefer? Put a big *E* on the line for them. If there is a mismatch, consider a few suggestions for how to shift the balance toward a little more playfulness. Or, if you need to tone it down, consider the next section on civility for some ideas.

Wendy: Dave is the playfulness expert in our family and hands down the hardest worker of any of us. Thanks to him, each of our kids has developed an ability to have fun along with a solid work ethic. For Dave, the two are closely related. Dave is certainly able to put in long hours at thankless work when necessary, but he also gets a huge kick out of much of what he does. He thinks the process of creating a new presentation or engaging a challenging business problem is fraught with fun. I learned early on that Dave was both hardworking and playful, but we were married for several years before I realized he was also funny. Maybe that says more about me than it does about him, but I honestly don't think Dave was always that funny. He developed his sense of humor to become a better teacher and a better person. He works at being funny, and sometimes he bombs. He doesn't let that stop him. When he finds a good one-liner, like all good comedians, he uses it again. He watches good comics in action. Not everyone is a natural at humor and playfulness, but most of us can get better at humor if we nurture it a little, see it as valuable, and lose a few of our inhibitions about what others will think of our beginning efforts.

How would you rate yourself on the humor and playfulness scale (1 to 10)? If you see room for improvement, it might be helpful to examine your attitudes about humor and fun. Fill in the following:

When I was a kid, I thought people who were playful were

The thing that makes me nervous about humor is

I would be more fun if

The arena where I could use more playfulness is

I think people who are funny are actually

_____

People get hurt by humor when

_____

I have been hurt by joking or humor when

_____

To be more playful I would need to

_____

I am funniest when

_____

The person who would most appreciate it if I lightened up is

_____

I could show this person my lighter side by

_____

Learn anything? Has your sense of humor been injured by ridicule or excesses? If so, what have you also learned about how humor can help without hurting? Have you seen people victimized by humor so that it has turned you off? If so, it may be time to collect the baby back from the bathwater and reinvest in your lighter side. Have you channeled your playfulness too narrowly? If so, it might be time to let more people see this side of you. Does your humor become mean-spirited, overly sarcastic, or crude? See if you can develop other aspects of your humor repertoire.

Consider who in your organization is great at humor and playfulness while still being a credible and contributing employee. How does he or she pull this off? What can you learn from this person?

Wendy: I'm not as good at humor as Dave, but I believe in the power of play. In my work as a psychologist I often invite adult clients to experience working in trays of sand, using miniatures to create whatever they like. Sand tray therapy is a powerful educational technique as well, helping people express without words what the nonverbal and most creative part of the brain knows but cannot articulate. The great psychologist Carl Jung once said, "Often the hands will solve a mystery that the intellect has struggled with in vain." This is true for big grown-up problems, not just little-kid problems, but big grown-ups often consider play beneath them. When I can get people to simply play in the sand and then tell me about their creations, they are often stunned at what they learn that they had no idea they knew. And this learning usually sticks far better than word learning alone.

Play has many uses for creative problem solving and innovation. Not only can we play directly at solving problems or imaginative innovation by drawing, crafting, or just manipulating objects, but sometimes taking a break from a pressing problem to go bat a ball around or knit for a while will allow creative solutions to kick in.

Pick up that pencil once again and number your piece of paper from 1 to 5. How could you enhance the atmosphere of appropriate humor, fun, and playfulness as a leader in your work setting? If nothing comes to mind, make this a group brainstorming exercise and see what others come up with.

Some possibilities:

○ Smile and laugh more.
○ Have your next team meeting with everyone sitting on the floor.
○ Give everyone poker chips to reward one another for going the extra mile.
○ Tell funny stories on yourself.
○ Give out prizes for the happiest desk or the most unflappable response to an irate customer.
○ Use window crayons and markers to brainstorm or draw solutions on the windows.
○ Wear costumes for Halloween and hand out candy.

Civility

Recently we spent a night at a posh private club in New York City as guests of a friend. We giggled at the list of stuffy rules: no flip-flops, no tennis shoes, only jackets and ties in the lobby or dining areas, no talking on cell phones or using computers in public spaces. But as we went to the breakfast buffet all scrubbed and suited, we couldn't help noting the air of . . . well . . . civility and delight. We got into a conversation with the waiter, an older man who talked and looked like Rocky Balboa's hard-nosed manager, who had worked at the club for 15 years and loved it. "Why?" we wondered. "Because the people here are just so *nice.*" As people who prefer gym clothes over all other attire and would go barefoot to the mall if we could, we are unlikely to buy a membership at a private club with a formal dress code anytime soon.

But we did find ourselves wondering if there is a time and a place to turn off the cell phone and put out some flowers. We did wonder if civility is a lost art worth cultivating.

In political debates where strongly held positions often lead to degrading others' points of view, civility has too often been replaced by hostility. As a result, the gears of the political process become stuck and no one benefits. Wise politicians can disagree without being disagreeable and have tension without contention. Political, organization, and personal civility shifts the debate from how we differ to how we can come to agreement, from how the other person is wrong to what we can learn from the other person, and from demeaning others to respecting them (even if we disagree).

Civility doesn't have to be stuffy or punishing, of course, and the type of civility we recommend should be neither. Instead of upturned noses or lots of rules, think writing notes of appreciation, acknowledging birthdays or personal events, offering little acts of kindness and respect, exhibiting basic politeness, smiling. Civility that is warm and friendly can help grease the skids of working at close quarters with people we don't always agree with. It won't work very well to expect sales reps to be sincere and polite to customers if we are not sincere and polite to them. Rate yourself (1 = low, 5 = high) on the following:

_____ I promptly and sincerely thank people for good work or extra effort, often in writing.

_____ I am appreciative and friendly to people who perform menial tasks.

_____ I say please, thank you, and "I goofed—I'm so sorry" to both colleagues and customers.

_____ I make it easy for others to tell me the truth because of how I respond.

_____ I attend weddings and funerals (literally and figuratively).

_____ I dress appropriately for the occasion.

_____ I avoid sexist, racist, or mean-spirited jokes or comments.

_____ I work to put people at ease around me.

_____ I listen to understand other people's point of view.

_____ I can disagree without being disagreeable and have tension without contention.

_____ I don't use anger or petulance to get my way.

The form civility takes in a Marine fighting unit may vary from that of a flower boutique, but civility has a place in both. Genuine civility generally brings out the best in people, who bring out the best in their colleagues and customers.

Ask your team members how they would rate you on the preceding criteria. How would they rate themselves? Do they think these are the right criteria for their work setting? What others would they substitute?

Customers and Delight

Our daughter Carrie, who does not consider herself a very techy person, recently decided to replace her outdated computer. She had put the decision off for a long time because both learning new technology and setting up a new computer intimidate her, and she has no idea where to begin in making computer-related decisions. She asked her brother, a statistician computer-geek, for advice. He talked her into an Apple, his personal favorite. She went to the Apple store, made her purchase, set up the computer, transferred all her files, and had a completely positive experience. She can't stop talking about how much she loves her new computer, how much fun it is to go back to the store for their computer classes, how hassle-free the purchase process was, and did we mention how much she loves her new computer?

We got curious about how a computer can meet the needs of both our tech-savvy son and our tech-avoidant daughter so well. As near as we can figure, both of them find a simple sense of delight in a product that is both technically advanced and deliciously intuitive. The screen is beautiful. The experience is tactile and inviting. They don't have to stand in line at the store, because every sales rep carries a little credit card reader around his or her neck. The computer synchs with the phone. And have you seen the cool way the icons swell enthusiastically when you run the cursor over them?

Most companies that make a living by attracting customers want people to experience that sense of delight because they know it translates into customer loyalty. Customer delight, may come from store layout, product features, a great bargain, or attentive service, and customer delight is a constantly moving target, but if companies can deliver on delight, they can usually count on people to come back. Companies that deliver on delight can usually count on their pick of creative employees as well.

A study done many years ago at a large retail firm with thousands of stores found that every 10 points of increase in employee engagement translated into a 4-point increase in customer satisfaction. We anticipate a similar connection between employee delight and customer delight. As

238

leaders make room for employees to experience both big C and little *c* creativity, enjoy little pleasures, find work conducive to a sense of humor and playfulness, and practice civility, employee satisfaction can turn into customer satisfaction.

You may not be able to afford a fancy gym or day-care center for your employees, but a yoga class or a Ping-Pong table might fly. Salaries may be frozen, but someone could still thaw out the cookie dough. Delight doesn't have to mean expensive artwork or fancy furniture, and it is not something people have to wait for management to provide— as long as thoughtful leaders are opening up the windows to let a little delight blow through.

An Unexpected Lesson in Delight

When the Khmer Rouge, a totalitarian Communist regime, took over Cambodia in the late 1970s, they emptied the capital city of Phnom Penh of its 2 million inhabitants in a matter of hours, sending everyone to the country to work in rice fields and on farms in makeshift huts and with no training or provisions. An estimated 1.5 million of the 7.1-million-person population died from torture, starvation, disease, and forced labor during the five years of Khmer Rouge rule, probably half from execution, making it the most lethal government of the 20th century. Schools, hospitals, banks, communication systems, and industry all came to a complete halt, with intellectuals, professionals, the educated, those with leadership skill, and city dwellers among the most suspect and the first to be executed. Children were separated from parents and trained in torture. The oft-repeated phrase from the government to the populace was "To keep you is no benefit. To destroy you is no loss."

Teeda Butt Mam and her family were among those evacuated from the city and sent to the rice fields to eke out a meager existence. Despite being well-educated professionals, they survived by working hard, adapting skillfully, and carefully hiding their background. As they became more aware of the relentlessness of their oppressors and the impossibility of escape, however, Teeda became more and more despondent. Though suicide meant sure punishment to surviving family members, when Teeda's friend was raped brutally and repeatedly until she died, Teeda began plotting her own death. Life had lost all meaning, and she felt dead inside. The months and years of horror and exhaustion seemed impossible to endure any longer, even for the sake of her mother and siblings. But then the story takes an unusual turn. Teeda states:

> Then, unexpectedly, on my way to the rice fields one morning, I glanced up, just as the sun rose over the paddies. The sheer beauty of heavy ripening rice silhouetted against the glorious orange sky took my breath away. A massive, plodding buffalo moved across the scene, giving a sense of the continuity of life from former times to now—an instant lesson in patience and perseverance. All nature affirmed that some things were beyond Angka Loeu's [the Khmer Rouge's] power to control. Neither sunrise nor storm, neither cloud nor wind nor bamboo, nor I, would be controlled by Angka. Angka Leou was not omnipotent. I felt—for the first time in months—that life might still hold something worthwhile.[4]

A tiny moment of delight, of beauty, declaring that "life might still hold something worthwhile," held Teeda steady through this moment of crisis and gave her a memory that held her through many others. She and her family eventually escaped Cambodia and started a new life in the United States.

If a small moment of delight can bring hope to someone in such circumstances, affirming that life is a precious gift even under the hand of unspeakable oppression, surely such moments can bring meaning to those of us with much less to overcome, much more to live for.

Summary: Leadership Actions to Foster Delight
- See and test the connection between employee delight and customer loyalty.
- Find ways to delight yourself at work and encourage your employees to find delight through:
  - Creativity
  - Pleasure
  - Humor/playfulness
  - Civility

CHAPTER 10

Implications for Executives, Human Resources, and Individuals

o, how do the seven principles and actions of *abundant organizations* apply to business executives leading organizations, to human resource professionals who work to institutionalize these ideas, and to individuals who seek meaning from the work they do?

Two Cases

Rodney Smith is the president of a small liberal arts university in rural Virginia. The idyllic campus was purchased about 15 years ago from a failing finishing school for girls, with the idea of creating a small Eastern mission-based university for members of the Church of Jesus Christ of Latter-day Saints—Mormon kids who more typically head to church- or state-run colleges in the West. Southern Virginia University has grown slowly under its current business model, and it is now home to about 650 students—about 400 shy of capacity. President Smith and his faculty and staff are passionate about their mission and deeply proud of their accomplishments: on average, entering students come in at about the 68th percentile academically and leave at the 93rd, with 55 percent going on to graduate programs. The students also graduate in less time, are significantly more satisfied with almost every aspect of their college experience, and are better prepared for jobs and graduate schools than comparable students attending competitor schools.

Southern Virginia University is ringing wet with meaning and organizational abundance. Like many start-ups, it faces inevitable financial struggles. Small, more expensive than its competitors, and in a remote location, SVU faces a constant uphill battle to pay the bills and come to the attention of prospective students. President Smith's business challenge is not about how to motivate employees with a compelling vision, great colleagues, challenging opportunities, or a positive work environment; SVU is already steeped in all the drivers of meaning. His task is to convincingly share with potential students and donors the particular world of meaning he and others have created so compellingly and to ground that meaning in fiscal disciplines and organizational capabilities to sustain it. Like many start-ups or purpose-driven enterprises, meaning is at the heart of SVU's very existence, but alone it will not be sufficient to ensure its success.

At perhaps another extreme would be a large business conglomerate in existence for a long time. We recently rented a car from an airport kiosk of just such a large national agency. While waiting for the paperwork to be processed, we asked a young employee standing nearby how she felt about her job. She candidly but somewhat sheepishly reported that she liked all the downtime when she could catch up on her favorite TV shows. A second, older woman who had apparently been there much longer was busy processing our rental documents, overheard our question, and volunteered *her* answers: she really liked chatting with customers, adding that she learned a lot from people she talked with. When Dave asked her if she had a bigger car available that might fit him better, she thought carefully about the available options and made a good recommendation; redid the paperwork without a grumble; gave us quick, accurate directions to the small, distant town we were headed to; and gave us clear, intuitive instructions for finding our car.

Working at a rental car kiosk is not exactly a job fraught with meaning, nor did the younger employee seem to need a compelling vision or challenging growth opportunity to get her to show up for work that day. She was content with a paycheck and the chance to watch TV. The question is, will she last? Will she attract and retain long-term customers? Will the agency's investment in training her pay off in their bottom line? Our guess would be that unless she can find more meaning in her work—as her more seasoned colleague seemed to have done—she will neither endure long nor contribute significantly to the company's success. Nor will it have much impact on hers.

Organizations face different challenges around meaning. Leaders of start-ups may put their stake in the ground precisely because they are hungry to fill a niche they care about and invest it with their passion and energy. They have plenty of meaning, but they need to find ways to communicate that meaning to stakeholders and support it with sound business practices. Leaders in established companies with proven track records and ingrained business practices may struggle more to keep their founding meaning fresh and growing, invest it with the energy and skill of established employees, and communicate it compellingly to new hires. And many companies line up somewhere in between on all these dimensions.

In this final chapter we will review why meaning is a crucial foundation for organization capability in all types of businesses and how top leaders, human resource professionals, and employees can create—returning to our original definition of abundant organizations—work settings in which individuals coordinate their aspirations and actions to create meaning for themselves, value for stakeholders, and hope for humanity at large.

The *Why* of Meaning at Work

In either personal therapy or leadership coaching, we generally start with a "presenting problem." In personal therapy the presenting problem might be symptoms of depression or anxiety, addiction, marital discord, or learning problems. For business leaders, this presenting problem might be a business challenge like loss of market or customer share, falling stock price, the need for more revenues in emerging markets, low customer service scores, technology changes in the industry, loss of key talent, or the need to grow through new markets or innovative products. To adequately address the presenting problem, one must identify and resolve its underlying causes. Treating only symptoms delivers only short-term gains that do not become sustainable solutions.

We believe that the underlying cause of many presenting problems in business today is a deficit of meaning. Our logic:

○ Presenting problems generally show up as an organization's *inability to respond to external requirements.* Presenting problems might be:

  ● Inability to meet customer needs—evidenced by falling customer share, market share, or customer service scores

  ● Losing investor confidence—evidenced by lower financial returns or lower stock values

  ● Poor community reputation—evidenced by erosion of brand confidence or inability to attract or retain employees

○ Underlying causes of these presenting problems are *lagging organization capabilities.* An organization capability is what the organization is good at and known for, such as the ability to:

  ● Change quickly

  ● Innovate

  ● Serve customers

  ● Operate efficiently

  ● Collaborate and build teams

  ● Learn

  ● Manage risk

○ An organization's capabilities are a collection of the *competencies and commitment* of individual employees. Organizations do not think or act; people do. When people think and act in a skilled, cohesive way, organization capabilities follow.

○ Individual competencies (ability to do the work) and commitment (willingness to do the work) are sustained and leveraged when employees see how their work makes a genuine *contribution* to people and causes they care about (finding meaning in the work).

To reverse this logic:

○ Employees' ability to find meaning in their work lever-
  ages and sustains their competencies and commitment.
○ The collective competence and commitment of employees creates organization capabilities.
○ These capabilities address the presenting problems
  facing organizations today, leading to sustained organizational success.

Employee meaning is, therefore, a lead indicator of not
only organizational abundance but also organizational prosperity. **Why** meaning? Because meaning has both inherent
value to individuals and market value to companies. Leaders
who diagnose, invest in, and improve meaning address
underlying causes, not symptoms, so their solutions endure
beyond quick-fix activities.

The *How* of Meaning

Leaders help employees find meaning at work as they learn
and apply the seven drivers of meaning we have presented.
These seven drivers tap into the inherent value or meaning
people generally find in:

○ Evolving their identity by using their personal values and
  strengths at work
○ Staying grounded in a purpose and a direction that con-
  nects personal drives to a common good
○ Enjoying satisfying relationships where they feel
  respected and attached

○ Creating positive work environments that sustain their productivity

○ Tackling challenges that invite growth and innovation

○ Finding value even in setbacks as they learn and bounce back

○ Appreciating the daily delights of civility, creativity, humor, playfulness, and pleasure

The **why** and **how** of meaning have implications for (1) leaders at all levels of a company, (2) human resource professionals, and (3) individual employees. All three can use these meaning drivers throughout an organization to promote both *personal values* and *bottom-line values*.

Leadership Implications

Our primary audience throughout this book has been leaders. Leaders set the tone for their organizations. Leaders make choices and investments that determine how organizations work. Leaders model what others follow. Sometimes employees consciously choose to follow their leader's intentional directives; other times the leader's behavior provides subtle cues about what is permissible or expected. When leaders focus on meaning-making activities, employees more readily sense that their experience at work matters to someone and that their contribution is valued.

Leaders at all levels can help make meaning happen.

Boards of Directors

The primary task of a board of directors is to monitor and ensure fiscal responsibility to shareholders. Some argue that organizations should also demonstrate social responsibility as an end in itself, even if doing so ignores profitability. While we admire the intent of this work, we believe it does not reflect the reality of competitive organizations. Competitive organizations that are socially responsible and make people feel good but don't serve customers and investors simply will not (and should not) survive. Even not-for-profit organizations succeed and survive only by delivering value to communities and constituents. But we don't have to rely on a social conscience to justify spending time building meaning. Research (reviewed in Chapter 1) compellingly suggests that meaning making for employees can be money making for shareholders. Employees who find meaning in their work have more positive attitudes, which in turn predict not only employee retention but also customer attitudes and shareholder confidence. If boards are serious about sustained financial success, they will attend to the creation of meaning. As shareholder representatives, boards often oversee financial results, product innovations, strategic choices, and customer satisfaction; we suggest boards also assess leadership depth, talent processes . . . and employee meaning.

To track meaning, boards pay attention to both formal indicators and informal observations. Retention of key talent, productivity indices about company outputs per unit of employee input, or employee survey scores on the meaning dimensions we reviewed in Chapter 2 each may be used to assess the extent to which employees find meaning at work. Board members may also use informal observations to track a sense of employee meaning. They may observe:

○ How employees treat outsiders (customers, board members, guests) who visit the company

- How employees show pride in their work setting (e.g., in cleanliness)
- What employees want to talk about when asked about their work
- How much employees use the products or services the company offers
- How many company symbols employees use
- What reputation the company has with outsiders

None of these queries or observations is perfect, and if employees are coached overtly to parrot the "right" answers or put on a show, these measures will become meaningless. But board members who ask, listen, and accept the answers given can get a feel for the degree of organizational abundance of a company. Board members who attend to employee signals and who openly discuss meaning making help connect social consciousness with sustainable economic success.

C-Suite Executives (*C* for Chief, as in Executive, Financial, Technology, Marketing, or Human Resource Officer)

Senior executives model and monitor their organization's level of abundant or deficit thinking. They live in glass houses, and their words and actions are scrutinized and mimicked. Senior leaders model a commitment to meaning by communicating, personalizing, and tracking meaning at work.

In formal settings like board meetings, annual reports, websites, performance reviews, training programs, and monthly staff meetings, leaders communicate priorities by what they spend time on and how they work through issues. In informal hallway conversations, leaders signal what matters most to them. When leaders are transparent about not only what is happening but also how they feel about it, when they face difficult issues head-on, and when they connect the creating of meaning to the making of money, they legitimate employee efforts to attend to and discover meaning at work. Leaders who share positive *affect* have positive *effect*.

Senior leaders personalize meaning and spread it around by sharing their aspirations and helping others do the same. A new president of a large state university began his first senior management retreat by asking everyone to tell a story about why he or she worked there. People talked about how education had enriched their personal lives, how their parents had sacrificed to provide them with schooling, how education had helped their children or siblings progress and contribute, or how they felt when they personally experienced students' learning and growth. These touching personal stories captured the shared identity and purpose of the university, reminding leaders why they did the work they did. The stories formed a foundation of meaning and shared vision that lent legitimacy and urgency to subsequent discussions of budget, curriculum, procedures, and staffing. When senior executives share how they feel about their work, they build a foundation of meaning that grounds their organizational efforts.

Communicating and personalizing meaning is not enough. Senior executives must help their organization turn aspirations into actions to sustain that meaning foundation. If the organization's values and goals are lauded but not materialized, meaning dissipates quickly.

Senior leaders need not only advocate and institutionalize meaning but also audit it. In addition to financial, customer, and organization reviews, leaders might ask questions such as these:

○ How do you feel about the work you do?

○ How do customers feel as they receive the outcomes of your work?

○ How do you use your strengths and values at work, and how often?

○ How do you see your work contributing to things you care about?

○ What are you learning about yourself in this job?

○ How do you explain what you do at work to your closest friends and family?

○ How much energy and passion do you feel for your work?

These questions focus on the emotion, values, and meaning inherent in work. They legitimate conversations about meaning at work. Of course, executive openness and accessibility will accentuate the grumbling of the disaffected, but thoughtful executives can use this to forestall bigger problems and make course corrections, as well as to ferret out more positive patterns. Sometimes listening comes from face-to-face employee visits in town hall meetings, at site visits, or on employee road shows. With technology, leaders can also get a sense from blogs, Web chat rooms, and employee networks. In all these listening posts, it is critical not to over- or underreact. It is also crucial not to "teach to the test" (rewarding the "right" comments rather than allowing comments to reflect real feelings). As leaders move around asking about meaning, they will raise awareness and accountability among others for its creation. In addition, senior executives can do organization meaning audits using the questions we laid out in Chapter 2 to determine whether their organization encourages meaning in each of the seven dimensions.

Leaders as Models

People say that charity begins at home. The same is true for meaning. To become a leader who shapes and creates meaning for others, start with a personal meaning audit:

○ How do I feel about my work?
○ What aspects of my job are the most meaningful to me?
○ What am I trying to accomplish that feels connected to a greater good I value?
○ Which of the seven drivers of meaning matters most to me?
○ Which of the seven drivers of meaning could I invest in to make a difference in how I experience my job?
○ What could I do in the next 30 to 90 days to help myself and my employees find more meaning in our work?

A leader's small meaning-promoting acts can enhance a sense of personal meaning. When budget cuts at one company meant eliminating snacks at corporate off-sites, the top executive personally baked cookies to pass around at the next retreat. In another company, a leader wrote personal thank-you notes to those who made unique contributions to a product or customer success. Another executive observed special events (birthdays, work anniversaries, children's graduations, funerals) with personal cards or notes. Another wrote gratitude letters to employees' significant others (spouses, partners, children, parents) to personally acknowledge the employees' good works. Such small and simple actions signal a sense of sharing values and of valuing employees. This is not to suggest in any way that a leader has to be every employee's best friend or that pragmatic financial issues be taken lightly. But the leader who attends to making meaning will likely find more support in meeting financial, customer, and other business goals as well.

Leaders communicate both formally and informally the things that matter most to them. When communications include not only facts but feelings, leaders can touch hearts as well as minds. At the large state university off-site where the president invited stories about why people cared about education, he gave each leader a Newberry Award–winning children's book and invited them to give the book to a child they knew. They were asked to write a personal note to this recipient to explain why learning mattered to them. This symbolic act helped them directly experience the joy of sharing the value of learning with someone they cared about. The university off-site ended with a video of current students telling their stories of how the university had helped them. Sharing customer experiences with a company's products or services helps employees connect with the impact of their work on real people—always a meaning builder.

Human Resource Implications

Dave has spent much of his career figuring out how to build human resource (HR) systems that deliver value—both inside the company to employees and managers and outside the company to customers, investors, and communities. He has helped focus HR on the outcomes or value it creates for others rather than on internal HR activities and practices. HR work that focuses on adding value becomes a means for leaders to sustain desired results. Dave is frequently asked why he chose to invest in HR. His response is simple: HR practices form the infrastructure that makes sustained organizational success possible.

Early in his career, Dave facilitated versions of a t-group, where members of a team got together over a weekend to share their personal feelings about work, each other, and the company. Late Saturday night, as fatigue set in, people's defenses often fell, and they tended to open up and be honest with each other, sometimes to the point of rudeness. Often a false sense of genuine emotional intimacy resulted. Unfortunately, this temporary intensity of sharing real feelings was frequently lost by Monday morning, when they all returned to work and the organization patterns they had established. Dave realized that sustained change did not come through emotive weekends but through institutionalized HR practices around recruitment, promotion, development, compensation, communication, and organization design. When these systems were changed, organization capabilities emerged that outlasted any single event or leader.

If employee meaning is a lead indicator of organization capabilities, financial results, customer service, and community reputation, it should also be a key outcome of good HR work. HR practices related to (1) people, (2) performance, and (3) organization can be designed to create and sustain meaning.

People Practices

Meaning should be a key consideration when hiring, training, developing, promoting, or outplacing employees. Hiring people who are technically competent and intellectually committed is not enough. Leaders and HR professionals should also examine the fit between the worker's values and passions and the job hired for. We have discussed under identity, purpose, and the nature of work signals that suggest employees are coming to work with not only their brains, hands, and feet, but also their hearts and souls. In monitoring these signals it is important to remember that many wonderful, contributing employees are not demonstrative extroverts who wear their passion for work on their sleeve. Signals may vary from person to person and should be used as just that—signals—not as ends in themselves to be rewarded or punished.

Training and development opportunities for employees should be initiated by both management (so employees acquire skills to do their work well) and employees who desire to learn and grow. Career moves should include consideration of what the employee feels passion about. Moving into a more senior position for the sake of salary and status alone does not always lead to sustained motivation. Employees are more likely to sustain energy and passion for their career moves if their signature strengths match their new roles. When it is necessary to let someone go, it should be done with care and concern, so that those who remain feel there is justice in the process.

Performance Practices

Total reward systems begin with clear expectations for both work outcomes (financial or customer results) and the behaviors that lead to them (such as the seven meaning drivers we have identified). Money is a big motivator, often a primary motivator. But money often has as much value as a symbol of importance or prestige as it does in buying power itself. Nonfinancial rewards like work flexibility, growth opportunities, access to valued relationships, and positive work environments are frequently at least as important as money in shaping employee meaning.

Organization Practices

Over time, organizations become institutionalized through their policies, structures, and physical settings. HR can also shape work policies and practices to support employees. We have seen companies offer:

o Concierge services to help employees with daily logistics
o A speaker series where employees could hear industry thought leaders
o Tutoring services where employees help other employees' children with homework
o Venture capital advice for employee spouses who wanted to start their own business (side note: when spouses used the business advice, the employee almost always stayed with the company)

Leaders can and should turn to their HR professionals to help design and deliver HR practices that instill meaning, linking these practices to presenting business problems. To promote meaning making, HR can architect choices, coach leaders on intended and unintended consequences of their actions, facilitate the processes of change, perform meaning audits, and help craft an employee value proposition that focuses not just on the terms and conditions of work but also on the emotional appeal and opportunities for contribution that the work provides.

HR practices institutionalize good intentions. Most of Dave's work has focused on creating and sustaining customer and investor outcomes of HR, and the creation of employee meaning is both a lead indicator of these outcomes and a valued outcome in and of itself.

Employee Implications

The importance of meaning to the next generation came into sharp focus in the spring of 2009 when almost half of the M.B.A.s graduating from Harvard Business School took a pledge to "do no harm," "serve the greater good," and "act with the utmost integrity." While symbolic more than binding, this ambitious pledge sent a clear signal about the hopes and ambitions of a talented and capable elite group. They expect work to make a difference for good in the world, they expect to make a difference at work, and presumably they expect work to make a difference to them. We see this social responsibility pledge as a worldwide tsunami with more and more business-oriented students wanting to both make money and do good.

In a very different setting, a colleague shared how he applied some of the concepts presented in this book with an entirely different audience:

> Last week I used your ideas (with some modification) to youth who are sentenced in a Detention Center. Their ages run from 10 to 18 years old. I first showed them pictures of several famous people—leaders and celebrities—and asked them what attributes come to mind when they thought of each particular person. After a few minutes of discussion I had them think of a person they knew personally who has made a significant difference in their lives and who has helped them find meaning. I had them list their attributes. Some shared a great deal—it was very touching at times. I then told them to list

the characteristics of their "ideal significant person." This next part was a bit abstract and I was worried that it would not work. I then told them that the attributes they listed for the "significant person" exercise were really their values, the attributes that they could aspire to. I spent a long time on the idea that those attributes often become hidden under much baggage, but if they focused on bringing meaning into their lives, they could find it. They "got it." Finally, I asked them to recognize the meaning they bring to the world and their families. I saw tears and many who recognized that they had worth within them—maybe for the first time. These were boys who were in jail who now had something in their hand, affirmed by them, which said that they brought something to us all. By exploring how others gave them meaning, they found meaning in who they were. So thanks. Some CEOs will benefit greatly from your book—but for 20 boys in a detention center it made a tremendous difference.

The search for meaning applies equally to Harvard M.B.A.s with bright futures and young adults with tough histories trying to identify who they are in a complex world. While skilled leaders can help guide that search, it falls to individual employees to pick up the trail if leaders do not. Abraham Lincoln is often quoted, "Most people are about as happy as they make up their minds to be." We would tweak this a bit: "Most people find about as much meaning in their lives as they make up their minds to find."

Employees make many choices that can enhance meaning in their personal and professional lives. Some employees might drop out of the corporate world and live more simply. Others will invest deeply in their careers and their companies. Whether exploring options for a first job, a job change, or just the job they get up for on yet another Monday morning, employees can make more thoughtful meaning choices about their professional lives by considering the seven questions we have suggested:

- **What will I be known for?** How can I express my core values in my daily work? Which job, career, or life choice will build on my strengths and best match my identity with the organization brand?
- **Where am I going?** What impact do I want to make on what types of problems? Which job, career, or life choice will help me reach my goals and accomplish things that are important to me?
- **Whom do I travel with?** How do I build the skills of good relating? Which job, career, or life choice will help me build relationships that matter to me?
- **How do I build a positive work environment?** What can I do to make my work environment more conducive to my work style? Which job, career, or life choice will be pursued in a work setting that I personally enjoy?
- **What challenges interest me?** How can I calibrate the level of challenge to stay optimally engaged and make a significant contribution? Which job, career, or life choice will offer me opportunities to do work that is easy, energizing, and enjoyable for me personally?
- **How do I respond to disposability and change?** How do I do a better job of making what I have enough? Which job, career, or life choice will help me grow, learn, and develop resilience when facing change?
- **What delights me?** How can I make more room for pleasure, playfulness, creativity, and living in the moment? Which job, career, or life choice will bring a sense of joy and delight to my personal and professional life?

We have asked these questions of hundreds of people facing choices among jobs, companies, and careers. These questions are timeless and work in both up and down markets to help people find a sense of meaning in their work lives. The seven meaning drivers also apply in families, neighborhoods, social groups, and volunteer associations. Wherever people work together to accomplish a shared goal, meaning matters.

A New Value Proposition

Traditional employee value propositions have focused on terms and conditions of work, often around pay and working conditions. While money will always matter, the new employee value proposition is also about meaning. In Chapter 1, we presented bleak statistics about the deficit that many people face in their personal and professional lives. In contrast to these deficits, this book explores how an abundance mentality focused on creating meaning can help employees in all kinds of circumstances find enough and to spare of what matters most. We believe that the heart of leadership is fundamentally about the creation of meaning and that leaders have a primary accountability to work with their employees to unleash it. A focus on meaning can yield employees who are more productive and committed, who build the organization's capacity to respond to business challenges, and who help their organizations succeed.

In up markets, when talent is scarce, meaning matters because employees are essentially volunteers who can choose where to allocate their time and energy. In down markets, some organizations experience a gratitude effect and get false positives on employee engagement scores from employees who gratefully compare themselves with less fortunate colleagues. But memories last longer than recessions. Employees who felt mistreated or taken advantage of during the down markets may look elsewhere when options open up. Companies that succeed at helping employees find meaning in downturns often create a cadre of resilient and motivated contributors who will be the problem solvers and innovators of future success.

We have had a number of candid conversations with leaders and employees at all levels about the changing role of leadership in today's business world. Often what we sense is increased cynicism. People distrust leaders who make personal gain more important than organizational and societal responsibility. Some will shy away from leadership opportunities because of this cynicism or because the price and risks of leadership feel too high in a transparent world, where leaders' privacy is lost to YouTube and leader decisions are debated endlessly on blogs and talk shows. There is an increasing and pressing need for good and great leaders at all levels of organizations and society—leaders who not only deliver results but also foster meaning, whose leadership agendas include both fiscal responsibility and social responsibility, who organize to both solve existing problems and imagine new possibilities. Leadership is a noble stewardship.

Meaning should be a real option for every worker who values it, and not just in not-for-profit organizations that have been its traditional province. Whether our future employees are graduating from the Harvard Business School or the local detention school, meaning matters. It matters not only for the profit of investors and the needs of customers but also for the hearts and souls of the millions of people who get up and go to work every day. Delivering on that hope is one of the most important opportunities facing business today.

Leadership Identity Challenge

With rapid technological, demographic, political, and social change, organizations scramble to align employee strengths into a coherent organization identity that responds to evolving customer and societal requirements. Great leaders help individuals align their personal strengths with the organization identity (firm brand) and with customer expectations.

Summary: *Leadership Actions to Build an Identity*

o Help employees become more aware of their signature strengths through assessment, conversation, observation, and assignment

o Define your organization's required strengths (or capabilities) by doing a capability audit

o Make sure that employees' strengths serve the organizational capabilities they are hired to build

o Define your key customers and investors and determine their expectations of you

o Connect the identity of the individuals and organizations to the customers they serve, building on strengths that strengthen others.

Leadership Purpose Challenge

In a world of information overload and centrifugal goals, employees and organizations often spin away from their basic sense of purpose and direction. Great leaders recognize what motivates employees, match employee motivators to organization purposes,and help employees prioritize work that matters most.

Summary: Leadership Actions to Articulate a Purpose

o Help employees recognize what motivates them (insight, achievement, connection, empowerment)
o Match the employees' motivation with the organization task they are assigned to perform
o Create an organization aspiration that declares a socially responsible agenda and translates that agenda to individual action
o Help employees satisfice in those tasks that are worth doing poorly and prioritize tasks that are important to do well.

Leadership Relationship Challenge

Despite increasingly competitive and isolating work settings and declining interpersonal skills, much work has to be accomplished with others and within teams. Great leaders help employees build skills for professional friendships between people and among teams.

Summary: Leadership Actions to Foster Relationships and Teams [Th]at Work

o Develop good friendships at work and encourage others to do so too
o Learn, teach, and model the skills of making and receiving bids, listening and self-disclosing, navigating proximity, resolving conflicts, and making amends
o Apply these skills to relationships between people and among teams

Leadership Positive Work Environment Challenge

Organizations develop unconscious patterns of how work is done that, left unattended, may lead to cynicism, disorganization, redundancy, or lethargy. Great leaders recognize and establish positive work environments that inspire employees, meet customer expectations, and give investors confidence.

Summary: Leadership Actions to Create a Positive Work Environment

o Pay attention to the work environment as patterns of how things are done
o Regularly monitor the work environment
o Pick two or three of the items from your diagnosis and focus on them
o Ask newcomers to your work environment their impressions of what is positive and what is not
o Make public statements about your commitment to shaping a positive work environment

Leadership Personalizing Contributions Challenge

Too often employees feel emotionally disconnected from the work they do; their work may capture their talents and time but not their heart and soul. Great leaders personalize work conditions so that employees know how their work contributes to outcomes that matter to them.

Summary: Leadership Actions to Ensure Personalized Contributions to Work Personalizing and Contributing Work

o   Learn what outcomes matter to employees; how does this job relate to their identity, values, and purpose
o   Help employees articulate the line of sight between what they do and the outcomes they value
o   Help employees discover the intrinsic value of their work and what they enjoy in the work itself
o   Shape work conditions and match employees to conditions that appeal to them (where, when, with whom, and how they work)

Leadership Growth, Learning, and Resilience Challenge

As changes compound and the risk of failure increases, people may fade, fail to adapt, and get demoralized, which leads to organization stagnation. Great leaders relish change and help employees grow, learn, and be resilient to bring new life to their organizations.

Summary: Leadership Actions to Facilitate Growth, Learning, and Resilience

o   Have a positive attitude about change, that you can learn from it and be resilient when facing it.
o   Learn how to generalize new ideas through self-reflection, experimenting, boundary spanning, and continuous improvement
o   Learn how to generalize, or share, new ideas by moving talent across boundaries, sharing information across boundaries, and building incentives to encourage shared behavior
o   Become resilient in the face of change by making the unspeakable speakable, turning what you know into what you do, and changing events into patterns

Leadership Delight Challenge

Partisanship sometimes affects organizations where there is more hostility than civility and where a we-they, win-lose, right-wrong, blame-and-shame mentality persists. Great leaders move away from hostility and intolerance toward multiculturalism through problem solving, listening, curiosity, diversity, and compassion and by bringing creativity, pleasure, humor, and delight into their organizations.

Summary: Leadership Actions to Foster Delight

o   See and test the connection between employee delight and customer loyalty.
o   Find ways to delight yourself at work and encourage your employees to find delight through creativity, pleasure, humor/playfulness, and civility

NOTES

Chapter 1

1. This research is summarized in: Ulrich, D., and N. Smallwood (2003). *Why the Bottom Line Isn't.* Boston, MA: Harvard Business Press.
2. These five companies are the only ones listed in both editions of the book *The 100 Best Companies to Work For* (1985 and 1993) and then on every list published in *Fortune* magazine since 1998.
3. Keynote address by Honorable Lyonchhen Jigmi Y. Thinley, prime minister of Bhutan, at the World HRD Congress 2010, Mumbai, 12 February 2010.
4. Bardwick, J. M. (2007). *One Foot Out the Door: How to Combat the Psychological Recession That's Alienating Employees and Hurting American Business.* New York, NY: AMACOM.
5. Marks, N., A. Simms, S. Thompson, and S. Abdallah. (2006). *The Happy Planet Index: An Index of Human Well-Being and Environmental Impact.* London, UK: New Economic Foundation. happyplanetindex.org.
6. Evans, V. (2008, February 29). *Depression Statistics—Just the Facts.* Retrieved January 22, 2008, from http://ezinearticles.com/?Depression-Statistics—Just-The-Facts&id=1017816. Kessler, R. C., W. T. Chiu, O. Demler, and E. E. Walters. "Prevalence, Severity, and Comorbidity of Twelve-Month DSM-IV Disorders in the National Comorbidity Survey Replication (NCS-R)." *Archives of General Psychiatry.* The World Health Organization. *The World Health Report 2004: Changing History,* Annex Table 3: Burden of Disease in DALYs by Cause, Sex, and Mortality Stratum in WHO Regions, Estimates for 2002. Geneva: WHO, 2004.
7. Kessler, R. C., W. T. Chiu, O. Demler, and E. E. Walters. "Prevalence, Severity, and Comorbidity of Twelve Month DSM-IV Disorders in the National Comorbidity Survey Replication (NCS-R)." *Archives of General Psychiatry,* 2005 Jun;62(6):617–27.
8. Andersen, A. E. (1995). "Eating Disorders in Males." In: Brownell, K. D., and C. G. Fairburn (Ed.), *Eating Disorders and Obesity: A Comprehensive Handbook* (pp. 177–187). New York, NY: Guilford Press. Spitzer, R. L., S. Yanovski, T. Wadden, R. Wing, M. D. Marcus, A. Stunkard, M. Devlin, J. Mitchell, D. Hasin, and R. L. Horne (1993). "Binge Eating Disorder:

Its Further Validation in a Multisite Study." *International Journal of Eating Disorders,* 13(2), 137–53. Yager, J., M. J. Devlin, K. A. Halmi, D. B. Herzog, J. E. Mitchell, P. S. Powers, and K. J. Zerbe (2000). "American Psychiatric Association Work Group on Eating Disorders: Practice Guideline for the Treatment of Patients with Eating Disorders (revision)." *American Journal of Psychiatry,* 1–39. Bruce, B., and W. S. Agras (1992). "Binge Eating in Females: A Population-Based Investigation." *International Journal of Eating Disorders,* 12, 365–73.

9. See World Wide Fund for Nature (wwf) report *Living Planet Report,* 2008. http://assets.panda.org/downloads/living_planet_report_2008.pdf.

10. See World Wide Fund for Nature (wwf) report *Living Planet Report,* 2008. http://assets.panda.org/downloads/living_planet_report_2008.pdf.

11. Fan, D., R. Wyatt, and K. Keltner (2001). "The Suicidal Messenger: How Press Reporting Affects Public Confidence in the Press, the Military, and Organized Religion." *Communication Research,* 28(6). Paxton, P. (1999). "Is Social Capital Declining in the U.S.? A Multiple Indicator Assessment." *American Journal of Sociology,* 105(1).

12. Gaines-Ross, L. (2008). *Corporate Reputation: 12 Steps to Safeguarding and Recovering Reputation.* New York, NY: Wiley.

13. Office for National Statistics. (2007, March 15). *Focus on the Digital Age.* Retrieved January 20, 2009, from statistics.gov.uk/focuson/digitalage.

14. Friedman, T. (2005). *The World Is Flat.* New York, NY: Farrar, Straus and Giroux.

15. In the 2000 census, approximately 30 percent of the U.S. population was "nonwhite," increasing in all states. Aguirre, A. (2003). *Racial and Ethnic Diversity in America: A Reference Handbook (Contemporary World Issues).* Oxford, UK: ABC-CLIO.

16. Gundling, E., and A. Zanchettin (2006). *Global Diversity: Winning Customers and Engaging Employees Within World Markets.* London, UK: Nicholas Brealey Publishing.

17. Twenge, J. M., and W. K. Campbell (2002). "Self-Esteem and Socioeconomic Status: A Meta-Analytic Review." *Personality and Social Psychology Review,* 6(1), 59–71.

18. Lancaster, L., and D. Stillman (2003). *When Generations Collide: Who They Are. Why They Clash. How to Solve the Generational Puzzle at Work.* New York, NY: HarperCollins.

19. Nielsen, A. C. (2007). *Television Statistics.* Retrieved January 20, 2008, from The Sourcebook for Science Teaching, csun.edu/science/health/docs/tv&health.html#tv_stats.

20. Putnam, R. (2000). *Bowling Alone: The Collapse and Revival of American Community.* New York, NY: Simon and Schuster. Putnam, R. D. (2007). "*E Pluribus Unum:* Diversity and community in the twenty-first century.

The 2006 Johan Skytte Prize Lecture." *Scandinavian Political Studies,* 30(2), 137–74. Retrieved January 20, 2009, from blackwell-synergy.com/ doi/full/10.1111/j.1467-9477.2007.00176.x.

21. Branham, L. (2005). *The Seven Hidden Reasons Employees Leave.* New York, NY: American Management Association.

22. *Employee Engagement Report.* (2008). Retrieved from blessingwhite.com/ EEE__report.asp.

23. 2006 Gallup study: Engaged employees inspire company innovation. *Gallup Management Journal.*

24. Gallup study: Engaged employees inspire company innovation. *Gallup Management Journal.*

25. YouGov (2009): yougov.co.uk.

26. Bernthal, P. (2004). Measuring Employee Engagement Development Dimensions International Inc. White paper.

27. Retrieved 20 January 2009 from divorcerate.org.

28. Seltzer, J. A. (1994). "Consequences of Marital Dissolution for Children." *Annual Review of Sociology, 20,* 235–66. Clark-Stewart, A., and C. Brentano (2007). *Divorce: Causes and Consequences.* New Haven, CT: Yale University Press.

29. Starker, S. (2002). *Oracle at the Supermarket: The American Preoccupation with Self-Help Books.* Piscataway, NJ: Transaction Publishers.

30. Salerno, S. (2005). *Sham: How the Self-Help Movement Made America Helpless.* New York, NY: Crown.

31. Bishop, B. (2008). No we didn't. Retrieved 5 March 2009 from slate .com/blogs/blogs/bigsort/archive/tags/2008+election/default.aspx.

32. Wilson, W. (1913). Swarthmore College, Swarthmore, Pennsylvania. 25 October 1913. Wilson, W. (1956). *The Politics of Woodrow Wilson: Selections from His Speeches and Writings.* New York, NY: Harper & Brothers. (Republished in 1970 by Harper & Row, Publishers, Inc.)

Chapter 2

1. There are many books on positive psychology: Seligman, M. E., and M. Csikszentmihalyi (2000). "Positive Psychology: An Introduction." *American Psychologist, 55,* 5–14. Seligman, M. (2004). *Authentic Happiness. Using the New Positive Psychology to Realize Your Potential for Lasting Fulfillment.* New York, NY: Free Press. Lyubomirsky, S. (2008). *The How of Happiness: A Scientific Approach to Getting the Life You Want.* New York, NY: Penguin.

2. Asplund, J., S. J. Lopez, T. Hodges, and J. Harter. (2009). *The Clifton StrengthsFinder® 2.0 Technical Report: Development and Validation* [technical report]. Lincoln, NE: Gallup.

3. Cameron, K. S., J. Dutton, and R. E. Quinn (2003). *Positive Organization Scholarship: Foundations for a New Discipline*. San Francisco, CA: Berrett-Koehler. Mroz, D., and S. Quinn. (2007). "Extraordinary Teams: Beyond High Performance." *Strategies*. http://competingvalues.com/competingvalues.com/wp-content/uploads/2009/07/Extraordinary-Teams-Beyond-High-Performance.pdf.

4. Savitz, A. W., and K. Weber (2006). *The Triple Bottom Line: How Today's Best-Run Companies Are Achieving Economic, Social and Environmental Success—and How You Can Too*. San Francisco, CA: Jossey-Bass.

5. Harter, J. K., and N. Blacksmith (2009). "Employee Engagement and the Psychology of Joining, Staying in, and Leaving Organizations." *Oxford Handbook of Positive Psychology and Work*. New York, NY: Oxford University Press. Sekerka, L. E., and B. L. Fredrickson (2009). "Working Positively Toward Transformative Cooperation." *Oxford Handbook of Positive Psychology and Work*. New York, NY: Oxford University Press. Richardson, J., and M. A. West (2009). "Dream Teams: A Positive Psychology of Team Working." *Oxford Handbook of Positive Psychology and Work*. New York, NY: Oxford University Press.

6. Wageman, R., D. A. Nunes, J. A. Burruss, and J. R. Hackman (2008). *Senior Leadership Teams: What It Takes to Make Them Great (Center for Public Leadership)*. Boston, MA: Harvard Business School Press. Hackman, R. (2008). *Leading Teams: Setting the Stage for Great Performance*. Boston, MA: Harvard Business School Press.

7. Gratton, L. (2009). *Glow: How You Can Radiate Energy, Innovation, and Success*. San Francisco, CA: Berrett-Koehler.

8. Mroz, D., and S. Quinn (2007). "Extraordinary Teams: Beyond High Performance." *Strategies*. http://competingvalues.com/competingvalues.com/wp-content/uploads/2009/07/Extraordinary-Teams-Beyond-High-Performance.pdf.

9. Ulrich, D. (1998). "Intellectual Capital = Competence × Commitment." *Sloan Management Review*, 15–26.

10. Stairs, M., and M. Galpin (2010). "Positive Engagement: From Employee Engagement to Workplace Happiness." *Handbook of Positive Psychology and Work*. New York, NY: Oxford Press.

11. Warren, S. (2010). "What's Wrong with Being Positive?" *Oxford Handbook of Positive Psychology and Work*. New York, NY: Oxford Press.

12. Warren, S. (2010). "What's Wrong with Being Positive?" *Oxford Handbook of Positive Psychology and Work*. New York, NY: Oxford Press.

13. Lyubomirsky, S. (2008) *The How of Happiness: A Scientific Approach to Getting the Life You Want*. New York, NY: Penguin.

14. Harter, J. K., and N. Blacksmith (2009). "Employee Engagement and the Psychology of Joining, Staying in, and Leaving Organizations." *Oxford Handbook of Positive Psychology and Work*. New York, NY: Oxford

University Press. Wright, T. A. (2010). "More Than Meets the Eye: The Role of Employee Well-Being in Organizational Research." *Oxford Handbook of Positive Psychology and Work.* New York, NY: Oxford Press. Stairs, M., and M. Galpin (2010). "Positive Engagement: From Employee Engagement to Workplace Happiness." *Oxford Handbook of Positive Psychology and Work.* New York, NY: Oxford Press.

15. Ulrich, D., and N. Smallwood (2003). *Why the Bottom Line Isn't.* New York, NY: Wiley. Ulrich, D., and N. Smallwood (2007). *Leadership Brand.* Boston, MA: Harvard Business Press.

Chapter 5

1. Fowler, J. H., and N. A. Christakis (2008). "Dynamic Spread of Happiness in a Large Social Network: Longitudinal Analysis Over 20 Years in the Framingham Heart Study." *British Medical Journal.* 337: a2338.

2. Rath, T. (2006). *Vital Friends: The People You Can't Afford to Live Without.* New York, NY: Gallup Press.

3. Ibid., 67–70.

4. Gottman, J. M. (2001). *The Relationship Cure: A Five-Step Guide to Strengthening Your Marriage, Family, and Friendships.* New York, NY: Three Rivers Press.

5. Tannen, D. (1986). *That's Not What I Meant!—How Conversational Style Makes or Beaks Relationships.* New York, NY: Ballantine Books.

6. Ibid., 20.

7. Tannen, D. (1990). *You Just Don't Understand: Women and Men in Conversation.* New York, NY: Ballantine Books.

8. Granovetter, M. S. (1973). "The Strength of Weak Ties." *American Journal of Sociology,* 6(78).

9. Goodwin, D. (2005). *Team of Rivals: The Political Genius of Abraham Lincoln.* New York, NY: Simon and Schuster.

10. Rath, T. (2006). *Vital Friends: The People You Can't Afford to Live Without.* New York: Gallup Press.

Chapter 6

1. Ackman, D. (2002). "Excellence Sought and Found." *Forbes,* October 10, 2002.

2. Malmendier, U., and G. Tate (2008). *Superstar CEOs.* Working paper from University of Berkeley.

3. Collins, J. (2004). *Good to Great: Why Some Companies Make the Leap and Others Don't.* New York, NY: HarperCollins.

4. Many people have written about servant leaders: Blanchard, K. (2003). *Servant Leader.* New York, NY: Thomas Nelson. Autry, J. (2004). *The Servant Leader: How to Build a Creative Team, Develop Great Morale, and Improve Bottom-Line Performance.* New York, NY: Three Rivers Press. Greenleaf, R., and L. Spears (2002). *Servant Leadership: A Journey into the Nature of Legitimate Power and Greatness.* Mahwah, NJ: Paulist Press.

5. Stewart, T. (1998). *Intellectual Capital: The New Wealth of Nations.* New York, NY: Broadway Business. Stewart, T. (2007). *The Wealth of Knowledge: Intellectual Capital and the Twenty-First Century Organization.* New York, NY: Doubleday Business. Sveiby, K. E. (1997). *The New Organizational Wealth: Managing and Measuring Knowledge-Based Assets.* San Francisco, CA: Berrett-Koehler.

6. Ulrich, D., R. Ashkenas, S. Kerr, and T. Jick. *The GE Work-Out.* San Francisco, CA: Jossey-Bass.

7. Nelson, B. (2002). *The 1001 Rewards and Recognition Fieldbook: The Complete Guide.* New York, NY: Workman Publishing. Nelson, B. (2005). *1001 Ways to Reward Employees.* New York, NY: Workman Publishing. Nelson, B. (1997). *1001 Ways to Energize Employees.* New York, NY: Workman Publishing. Kaye, B., and S. Jordan-Evans (2008). *Love 'Em or Lose 'Em: Getting Good People to Stay.* San Francisco, CA: Berrett Koehler.

8. This story comes from Raymond Schkolnem who was the head of HR for the business at the time.

9. Miller, J. (2003). *The Suggestion System Is No Suggestion.* Gemba Research. Retrieved from gemba.com/uploadedFiles/The%20Suggestion%20System%20is%20No%20Suggestion.pdf.

10. National Safety Council (1992). Accident facts. Chicago, IL: National Safety Council. Herman Miller, Inc. (2002). *Body Support in the Office: Sitting, Seating, and Lower Back Pain.* Herman Miller Inc. Retrieved from hermanmiller.com/hm/content/research_summaries/wp_Body_Support.pdf.

11. Herman Miller, Inc. (2001). *Lighting in the Workplace.* Herman Miller, Inc. Retrieved from hmeurope.com/WhitePapers/wp_Lighting_in_Wkpl.pdf.

12. Merck & Co, Inc. (2009). *Building a Positive Work Environment: Advancing the Dialogue Toward a Healthier Future.* Merck & Co, Inc. Retrieved from merck.com/corporate-responsibility/basics/employees/employees-benefits-compensation-training/home.html.

13. Conoco-Phillips. (2008). *Conoco-Phillips Company.* Retrieved from conocophillips.com/SusDev/ourpeople/promoting/index.htm.

14. Brisbane City Council. Joint City Council/Planning Commission Special Meeting. Meeting held 9 April 2007 in Brisbane, California. Minutes taken by Sheri Marie Schroeder, City Clerk.

15. Meraviglia, M., S. J. Grobe, S. Tabone, M. Wainwright, S. Shelton, H. Miner, and C. Jordan (2009). "Creating a Positive Work Environment Implementation of the Nurse-Friendly Hospital Criteria." *Journal of Nursing Administration*, 39(2), 64–70.
16. TSL Education Ltd. (2009). *Times Higher Education*. Retrieved from timeshighereducation.co.uk/hybrid.asp?typeCode=340&pubCode=1&navcode=98142.

Chapter 7

1. Connecting actions and outcomes comes from classic work called *expectancy theory*. In this theory, if an individual believes a task can be done (expectancy), if the individual sees a high probability that doing the task will result in a meaningful outcome (instrumentality), and if the outcome is valuable (valence), then the individual will commit more discretionary energy to the task. Vroom, V. (2005). "On the Origins of Expectancy Theory," in Smith, K., and M. Hitt. *Great Minds in Management: The Process of Theory Development*. Oxford University Press, 239–58.
2. Business Week (2006). Smashing the clock: No schedules. No mandatory meetings. Inside Best Buy's radical reshaping of the workplace. *Bloomberg L.P.*
3. There are a number of studies of antecedents of engagement and what employees want: Magnuson, D., and L. Alexander (2008.) *Work with Me: A New Lens of Leading the Multigenerational Workforce*, Personnel Decisions International. Morgan, L. (2004). Corporate Leadership Council (2004). *Driving Performance and Retention Through Employee Engagement*. Holbeche, L., and N. Springett (2004). "In Search of Meaning at Work" (report).
4. Kaye, B., and S. Jordan-Evans (2008). *Love 'Em or Lose 'Em: Getting Good People to Stay*. San Francisco, CA: Berrett Koehler.
5. Simon, H. A. (1957). *Models of Man: Social and Rational*. New York, NY: Wiley. Simon, H. A. (1978). "Rationality as a Process and Product of Thought." *American Economic Review*, 68, 1–16. Simon, H. A. (1983). *Reason in Human Affairs*. Stanford, CA: Stanford University Press.

Chapter 8

1. Clark, T. R. (2008). *Epic Change: How to Lead Change in the Global Age*. San Francisco, CA: Jossey-Bass.
2. Lawler, E., and C. Worley (2006). *Built to Change: How to Achieve Sustained Organizational Effectiveness*. San Francisco, CA: Wiley.

3. Zasky, J. (2009). "Going out of Business Tales: Learning from Inexcusable Business Failures." *Failure Magazine, LLC*. Retrieved from http://failuremag.com/index.php/site/print/going_out_of_business_tales.

4. Jarvis, J. (2009). *What Would Google Do?* New York, NY: HarperBusiness.

5. Ashkenas, R., D. Ulrich, T. Jick, and S. Kerr (1995). *Creating the Boundaryless Organization*. San Francisco, CA: Jossey Bass.

6. These individual competencies for organizational learning come from the combination of the organization architect and career architect tools by Lominger. In organization architect, one of the 16 organization capabilities deals with the ability to share information (cluster 7). Lominger then tied this organizational capability to the specific individual competencies most likely to make it happen.

7. The concepts on measures and rewards are drawn from Lawler, E. E. (1990). *Strategic Pay*. San Francisco, CA: Jossey-Bass. Kerr, S. (1988). "Some Characteristics and Consequences of Organizational Reward" in Schoorman, F. D., and B. Schneider (Eds.). *Facilitating Work Effectiveness: Concepts and Procedures*, Lexington, MA: Lexington Books.

8. Kearns, D. G. (2006). *Team of Rivals. The Political Genius of Abraham Lincoln*. New York, NY: Simon and Schuster. Donald, D. H. (1996). *Lincoln*. New York, NY: Simon and Schuster. McPherson, J. (2009). *Abraham Lincoln*. London, UK: Oxford University Press.

9. Carnegie, D. (2004). *How to Stop Worrying and Start Living*. New York, NY: Pocket.

10. See MADD.com, where those who are bereaved can share their stories and experiences to gain support.

11. Some of the 9/11 support groups include Adam's Angels, adamsangels.org; Long Island 9/11 Memorial, li911memorial.org; 9/11 Memorial Bracelets, http://nleomf.com/html/products/9100l, memorialbracelets.com; Pentagon Memorial Project, http://memorial.pentagon.mil; Reclaiming the Sky, reclaimingthesky.com; The Peter M. Goodrich Memorial Foundation, goodrichfoundation.org; Tuesday's Children, tuesdayschildren.org; Windows of Hope, windowsofhope.org.

Chapter 9

1. Bryan, M., J. Cameron, and C. Allen (1998). *The Artist's Way at Work: Riding the Dragon*. New York, NY: William Morrow.

2. Maisel, E. (1995). *Fearless Creating: A Step-by-Step Guide to Starting and Completing Your Work of Art*. New York, NY: Tarcher/Putnam.

3. Maisel, E. (1995). *Fearless Creating: A Step-by Step Guide to Starting and Completing Your Work of Art*. New York, NY: Tarcher/Putnam.

4. Criddle, J. (2004). *To Destroy You Is No Loss: The Odyssey of a Cambodian Family*. Auke Bay, Alaska: East/West Bridge Publishing House.

INDEX

ABOUT THE AUTHORS

Organizations exist to create value both inside to employees and outside to customers, investors, and communities. When internal leadership and human resource practices align to external expectations, organizations survive and thrive.

Dave Ulrich is a professor at the University of Michigan Ross School of Business and a partner at The RBL Group, a consulting firm focused on helping organizations and leaders deliver value. He studies how organizations build capabilities of leadership, speed, learning, accountability, and talent through leveraging human resources. He has helped generate award-winning databases that assess alignment between strategies, human resource practices, and HR competencies. His writing, teaching, and coaching have helped shaped the role of human resources in global organizations. His work has helped leaders both become more personally effective and build better leadership throughout their organizations. He has helped to redefine organizations more by the capabilities they deliver to customers and investors than by their structure and systems.

Dave has published more than 150 articles and book chapters and 22 books. He edited *Human Resource Management 1990–1999* and has served on editorial board of four professional journals, on the Board of Directors for Herman Miller, and on the Board of Trustees at Southern Virginia

University. He is a Fellow in the National Academy of Human Resources. He has won numerous lifetime honors and been consistently ranked among thought leaders in business and human resources. He has consulted and done research with over half of the Fortune 200.

Recent publications include:

Leadership in Asia (2009, edited book, published by McGraw Hill)

HR Transformation (2009, with Justin Allen, Wayne Brockbank, Jon Younger, and Mark Nyman, published by McGraw Hill)

Leadership Code (2008, with Norm Smallwood and Kate Sweetman, published by Harvard Business Press)

Companion for Strategic Human Resources (2008, with John Storey and Pat Wright, published by Routledge)

HR Competencies (2008, with Wayne Brockbank, Dani Johnson, Kurt Sandholtz, and Jon Younger, published by SHRM and RBL Group)

Leadership Brand (2007, with Norm Smallwood, published by Harvard Business Press),

Human Resource Value Proposition (2005, with Wayne Brockbank, published by Harvard Business Press)

*The Future of Human Resource Management (*2005, with Michael Losey, Sue Meisinger, published by Wiley & Sons)

Human Resources Business Process Outsourcing (2004, with Ed Lawler, Jac Fitz-enz, James Madden, published by Wiley & Sons).

Contact information: e-mail: *dou@umich.edu*, websites: *rbl.net and thewhyofwork.com.*

Humans are meaning-makers who find *inherent value* in making sense out of life. In addition to inherit value, meaning has *market value* in work settings. Making sense makes cents.

A licensed psychologist in private practice for twenty years, Wendy Ulrich brings a personal touch to corporate complexities. She focuses on helping leaders create meaning at work that contributes real value to employees, customers, and investors. Employees who find a why to work are motivated and productive co-developers of abundant organizations with enough and to spare of the things that matter most: creativity, hope, resilience, determination, resourcefulness, and leadership . . . all in the service of customer commitment and financial performance.

Wendy helps organizations build personal strengths and people skills to succeed: communication, problem-resolution, change, creativity, resilience, civility, forgiveness, and happiness. She speaks to thousands of people every year on these topics.

In addition to counseling and coaching of individuals, Wendy has provided training and consulting for such organizations as General Electric, the U.S. Army, Johnson & Johnson, and the United Way. She is the founder of Sixteen Stones Center for Growth (sixteenstones.net), offering seminar-retreats for individuals and groups on topics such as forgiveness, loss, and creating an abundant life. She has taught psychology and organizational behavior at the University of Michigan, Northrup University, and Brigham Young University and is a fellow and former president of the Association of Mormon Counselors and Psychotherapists.

Wendy holds a Ph.D. in education and psychology from the University of Michigan and an M.B.A. specializing in organizational behavior from UCLA.

Recent publications include:

Weakness Is Not Sin: The Liberating Distinction That Awakens Our Strengths (2009)
Forgiving Ourselves: Getting Back Up When We Let Ourselves Down (2008)

Contact information: e-mail: wulrich@rbl.net, websites: sixteenstones.net and thewhyofwork.com.